♦ A FIELD GUIDE TO ♦

AMERICA'S
HISTORY

• A FIELD GUIDE TO •

AMERICA'S HISTORY

By Douglass L. Brownstone

Illustrations by Staats Fasoldt

Facts On File, Inc.
New York, New York • Bicester, England

◆ A FIELD GUIDE TO ◆
AMERICA'S
HISTORY

Library of Congress Cataloging in Publication Data

Brownstone, Douglass L.
   A field guide to America's history.

   Bibliography: p.
   Includes index.
   1. Historic sites—United States—Guide-books.
2. United States—History, Local.   3. United States—
Description and travel—1960-   —Guide-books.
I. Title.
E159.B895   917.3'04927   82-7434
ISBN 0-87196-622-0

Printed in the United States of America

Dedicated to the memory of Jane Bostwick

◆ TABLE OF CONTENTS ◆

◆ ACKNOWLEDGMENTS ◆

Writing this book involved long hours of documentary research, most often conducted with a two-year-old daughter named Rebecca patiently tagging along. Thanks, Becky, for being such a great kid.

I couldn't have finished this work without the help of the excellent N.Y. State library system. Inter-library loan was a frequent lifesaver when research became snagged. Special thanks to the staff at the Ulster County Community College Library in Stone Ridge, N.Y. I also wish to thank Norman Brouwer, ship historian at the South Street Seaport Museum, for sharing his broad knowledge of waterfront development with me; Eleanora Schoenebaum, my editor, for her enthusiastic support of this project; my wife, Debbie, for being herself; and the many other people whom I've talked with about different aspects of this project during the last three years.

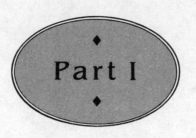

Part I

THE
LAND
TALKS

Today's landscape is the ultimate jigsaw puzzle. Many years of development have produced a seemingly chaotic jumble of buildings and artifacts that coexist in various states of preservation and clarity. The pieces of the puzzle are scattered through time as well as space and leave the casual observer with only tantalizing hints of the past. The overlay of twentieth century America is a dauntingly heavy veil.

Although individual restorations and designated historic sites can provide accurate glimpses of past landscapes, they remain curiously lifeless. Presented like particularly skillful holograms, they often give the impression that they alone survive in a sea of modernity. Fortunately the past is much too woven into the fabric of the countryside to be massively obliterated. All the clues that you need to sight across the years are there, ready to be used.

Anyone undertaking a personal expedition into the everyday history of his surroundings faces great demands. To develop a time-piercing vision you must bring an unquantifiable gift of imagination to your acquired knowledge and skills. A failure to do so can leave you dismally unsatisfied.

The study of historical methodology may mean you can coldly dissect layers of past life investing the landscape, but it certainly does not guarantee enjoyment. Dry catalogues of carefully time-lined artifacts and events are testimonials to tidily completed tasks, and little more.

The land around you is a living organism with memories inextricably linked to the histories of those who once lived there. It takes a subtle leap in spirit to bring the worlds of these elder neighbors into meaningful form. To see them as people, and chart the progress of their hopes and disappointments through the signs of their sojourns on the land, can help you to better appreciate the terms of your own tenancy, make the extraordinarily complex weaving of settlement and use more understandable.

Then too, the search itself is the sovereign cure for the maladies of boredom and complacency. Every excursion out your door can mean discovery and challenge. Each time another clue is uncovered that brings the past to life, there is a potent rush of satisfaction giving you energy for more.

To unearth the basic order that lurks under the surface of the tangled modern environment, it helps to make a great leap backward. Look at the land and try to ignore the buildings and roads that overspread it. Once your vision begins to tally with what the early settlers saw, the reasons for their subsequent actions become clearer.

Seeing the land with an undistracted eye can be difficult, to say the least. Your horizons may be circumscribed by tall buildings, trees, hills, and other such natural and unnatural barriers. A trip skyward offers the best perspective, but planes and helicopters are rather expensive and inefficient vehicles for acquiring an unrestricted view of the land. You are far better off sinking into a comfortable chair and turning your attention to a topographic survey map. (See Chapter 6, A Matter of Record.) With its clear and comprehensive picture as a guide to the land's features, you can begin to view the countryside with a settler's appraising eye.

1 ◆

WATERFALLS AND WATERWAYS

The words "New World" have been so well oiled by centuries of casual handling that they slip by the modern ear without stirring much emotional impact. They simply form an old-fashioned phrase which is occasionally used to distinguish the Americas from Europe.

The early settler found a commanding majesty in those same words. The New World was a very real and graspable place; a region of limitless land and prospects and wondrous unknowns. The contrast with the long-inhabited European landscape was inescapable and compelling. The immensity of the new continent defied the restrictive feudal pattern of land owned by the nobility and worked by servile peasants. Freeholds and individual fortunes awaited the pioneer who was willing to set himself against the wilderness.

Men and women spread across the countryside in a frenzied wave of settlement throughout the eighteenth and nineteenth centuries, but their enthusiastic progress was tempered by certain inflexible conditions. The homesteader, hacking out his own niche, could not take survival for granted. Those who did often disappeared without a ripple to mark their passing. Each westward-bound traveler had to survey the new land with an appraising eye. A correct judgment of the land's potential often meant the difference between success and bankruptcy, between survival and death.

Water attracted settlers with greater force than it ever exerted on the peach-tree divining rod held in a dowser's hand. Here's the place to set your roots and build a future, called every possible mill site. Follow my course and use my waters for the transport of your families and goods, tempted every waterway. The blandishments of cold, clear, never-failing springs were formidable and rarely ignored.

Head for water if you want to find the earliest sections of the settled landscape. Follow the line inked on your survey map or steer for the glint of a creek running swiftly down a steep valley. But go. Let your investigative gaze lead you to water as unerringly as it did the first settlers.

The first Europeans arriving in the New World looked at the impenetrable wooded countryside and simply followed standard explorers' procedure. They knew that rivers held more promise than the land. It was far easier to paddle or pole your way upstream and portage around rapids than to cut a roadway through the woods. Later settlers were sure to follow the routes of those pathfinders. Small communities sprang up along riverbanks, wherever a particularly attractive piece of land beckoned. Until the middle of the nineteenth century, when railroads began to cross the land, waterways served as the major funnels for the westward emigration. The advantages of water for travel and the transport of heavy goods were so predominant that artificial waterways were built to supplement natural ones. During the first half of the nineteenth century dozens of canals were dug to open up those sections of the country not blessed with navigable rivers. (See Chapter 7, Canals.)

Trail heads and jumping-off points for the few major overland routes west were invariably situated at the boundaries of the waterway network. The selection of Independence, Missouri, as the staging ground for both the Oregon and California trails was hardly coincidental. It sits at the precise point where the Missouri River abandons its direct western flow and heads north. The same pattern held true numberless times on the smaller and more variable canvas of local settlement.

Creeks and rivers that could never hope to support boat traffic were still lodestones for settlement, industry, and travel. Invariably they followed the contour of the land in their winding progress to a larger body of water, and in doing so they suggested fairly level overland routes to the interior. However, the potential of waterpower to drive machinery was an even greater enticement.

Sawmills and gristmills were essential to successful settlement, and suitable mill sites, where waterfalls or rapids could be harnessed, were always quickly claimed locations. You can be sure that the better mill sites in any region were the nuclei of early communities. Superior waterpower sites along navigable rivers or canals played a crucial role in the country's development. They attracted the major industries which ushered in the manufacturing age, and the massive transformation of the land that resulted. (See Chapter 13, Mills and Factories.)

Aside from transportation and power, water had other important roles to play in a homesteader's selection of land on which to settle. Cropland had to be well-drained to produce abundantly, and, ideally, alongside a source of water that could be used for irrigation in time of drought.

A reliable supply of drinking water for people and livestock was a prime consideration. In the eastern part of the country, the natural ground water was normally ample, and creeks or man-made wells sufficed except during extreme droughts. Even in the best areas, the specter of drought always lurked in the back of the inland farmer's mind. A guaranteed water supply made land far more valuable.

Springs not only cushioned against thirst, they had other sterling qualities as well. The superior quality of spring water, colder and clearer than any surface source, was appreciated wherever it was found. The mineral content of many springs was also prized for its medicinal qualities. Notable springs quickly gathered communities to their outlets and bestowed their names to the towns along with their waters.

2♦

THE SOIL'S STORY

For most of its history, America has been a nation of farmers, perpetually entranced by the lure of richer cropland over the next hill. The migration westward was fueled by an overmastering land hunger. Men and women claimed homesteads from forests and prairies with hand labor that seems incredible to the modern mind. Acres of timber were cut and cleared without the benefit of chain saws and tractors, the remaining stumps were pulled and the land was made ready for cultivation. No amount of work was too much as long as it resulted in land that could be owned, farmed, and built on.

Early farmers often had to make do with thin soil and rocky land. The areas open to them were limited by the frontier's border, and the ever-present threat of Indian attack was a potent deterrent to solitary moves into unclaimed and unknown countryside. Farm communities clustered together for support and often sought security on the high grounds of ridges and hills. Families working these poorly endowed holdings left them as soon as it was safe to seek richer territory. Farms bred farms as quickly as they did their pigs and corn. Soil that was none too fertile to begin with quickly wore out when it was subjected to intensive cultivation without renewal or respite. In Europe, the limited availability of arable land made conservation, fertilization, and crop rotation necessary items in a farmer's repertoire. These sensible and time-honored customs rarely made the passage across the Atlantic. Few farmers were willing to slave endlessly over one piece of land when there was a vast frontier of richer parcels waiting to be claimed. As soon as crop yields started to fall, it was time to pack up, sell, and move on. An active man could brag of wearing out several farms in his lifetime as he moved ever deeper into the country.

Flat land and rock-free soil were a farmer's dream, but it was not always realized. Early homesteaders in New England often had to settle for hardscrabble acreage that seemed to grow rocks in a greater abundance than any other crop. Stonewalls are often the only markers of land left for the richer pickings of the western frontier. These long, stretching rock boundaries are a sure sign of difficultly worked and laboriously cleared soil, the marks of the heavy and unwanted harvest that bedeviled the farmer working that land.

In the hilly east, flat fields were valley land, but farmers did not hesitate to move up the hillsides if the land could grow crops and was unoccupied. Small, sharply sloped fields that would not lend themselves to modern farm machinery presented few obstacles to the energetic farmer. A man relying on the slow and measured progress of draft animals to haul his plow took the hillside in stride.

The shapes of abandoned farm fields can give you a clue to their former uses. Long, narrow lots were cropland that witnessed the sweating progress of the farmer following an animal-drawn plow down its furrows. When tractors were introduced on the farm, they had trouble negotiating the sharp turns at the end of these relatively small fields and much greater expanses had to be cleared and planted for efficient cultivation.

Squarish fields, particularly those with rocky or broken terrain, were probably pasturage for the farmstead's livestock. The village commons of early settlements, which had held the community's livestock, were soon unable to handle the inundation of horses, pigs, sheep and cattle which increasing populations and prosperity brought. It became the farmer's responsibility to set aside a portion of his own land for his own animals, and fencing became an important part of community life.

As pioneering farmers moved west, they developed a keen eye for soil that promised the greatest yield. The tree cover of the virgin forest was a likely indicator of the soil's worth. The well-drained soil of "sugar tree lands" or other hardwood forests was nearly always preferable to the damp and clinging soil of "beech land." Whenever there was the slightest doubt, you were sure to find men hunkered down, carefully inspecting handfuls of soil to judge its promise.

Handfuls of dirt should be part of the checklist of analytical tools you use to read the land. To properly reap the historical harvest, the subject of soil fertility must concern you as much as it did the early farmer. The general potential of different areas can help you form an overall picture of the order in which the land was cleared, even though centuries of use and development may have drastically altered the soil's composition.

You'll find that a sensitivity to the soil's relative productivity will be of real value in your investigation of specific sites. The clues read in the earth of abandoned farmsteads and long-vanished factories can unriddle key parts of their past.

The signs you are looking for are anomalies in the regular pattern of the earth's makeup which show that the hands of men have disturbed the surface. The marks of continued usage remain for a very long time on the land, and an informed eye can read their clues. Soil compacted by the repeated pounding of feet or vehicles becomes barren land, impervious to life-giving rainfall. Topsoil removed from its rightful place leaves a scar that takes many generations to renew itself.

Aerial-photo interpreters are well aware of these facts. Outlines of prior development and significant differences in the vigor of plant cover can be seen with crystal clarity from the air even when they are largely invisible from ground level. One of the main ways to trace toxic waste dumps, for example, is through photo identification of their access roads, and the subtle messages of soil poisoning which spread across the land like festering wounds.

Your earthbound vantage point will give you access to signs of usage that are less dramatic but often still clear and intelligible. Roadways that carried decades of wagon traffic or canal towpaths that were host to thousands of mule teams will be very different patches of land than the surrounding neighborhood. For the plainest messages, look for signs when vegetation is at its least luxuriant. If you're in country where there is snowfall, the first dustings of the season will make old roadways and paths spring into instantly identifiable contrast.

Past industrial activity can yield additional soil clues long after the actual structures have vanished. Any slag heap or dump where chemical byproducts were let loose upon the land will leave a region where only stunted and extremely hardy plants are able to coax nourishment from the soil.

Mines and quarries leave scars that last for centuries because of the ruthless way they remove life-giving topsoil and expose the dense hardpan of the subsoil to the air. On a smaller and less dramatic scale, your probing gaze can use the same method of observation to unriddle the story of old farmsites as well.

That patch of light, sandy subsoil which is home to a few straggling plants by the old foundation should instantly suggest further investigation to you. Whenever a well was dug or a privy excavated, the carefully balanced natural composition of the soil was significantly altered.

3.

PLANT LANGUAGE

I t's all too easy to view the plants investing intriguing historical locations with a dismay that verges on downright hostility. Poison ivy patches, ranks of nettles, blackberry thickets, and a prickling and concealing array of similar annoyances can quickly dampen your investigative ardor.

Lurking in that vegetable army are friendly and illuminating presences that you should take the time to make the acquaintances of. Clues read in the undergrowth are sometimes the keys which first alert you to the presence of a site worth looking at.

When you think about it, it's certainly fitting that you pay close attention to the vegetation surrounding you. The people whose lives you're trying to understand were far more intimate with plant life than we are today. Farmers, frontiersmen, manufacturers and artisans of the nineteenth century, and earlier, all depended on the resources contained in the plants of the forest and field. The contempt and inattention our industrialized society exhibits for this knowledge is a recent and not necessarily permanent condition.

◆ TREES ◆

Tree lore was the centerpiece of the settlers' fund of plant learning. People knew which wood best suited which purpose—be it wagons, brackets, buttons, furniture, charcoal, fences, or countless other products. Every practical man knew the character of the trees in his neighborhood.

Trees should figure prominently in your own investigative arsenal. Their practical applications are fascinating, but they are not the elements which will commonly give you the most information. The virgin first-growth forests—both wooden cornucopia and vexing obstacles to the farmer in need of crop land—are long gone. Settlement took on the task of removing the seemingly inexhaustible forests of the eastern half of the country with reckless abandon. Farmers doggedly cleared new fields for cultivation, charcoal burners felled whole forests to fuel growing industries, sawyers, tanners, and a host of other workers performed their jobs only too well. By the 1870's most of the original tree cover had been completely stripped.

The woodlands which are so abundant today are nearly all second- and third-growth forests whose trees will never reach the size and quality of their predecessors. The few survivors of the practically universal clearcutting are the signposts that you're looking for. The demand for wood was so intense during the last quarter of the nineteenth century that any sizeable original specimens had to owe their survival to a special set of circumstances.

◆ BOUNDARY TREES ◆

A walk through any settled countryside will immediately bring you into contact with trees that are far more imposing than their neighbors. These gnarled and thickened veterans are commonly found flanking roadways, in the margins of fields, and spaced along the faintly marked courses of old fencelines. They serve as landmarks in the most basic and practical sense of the word.

When surveyors set about dividing the countryside into individual plots of land, they needed reference points for their written descriptions of the parcels. In a forested country there was nearly always a convenient tree ready to be incorporated into the metes and bounds of the property deed. That tree bore a charmed life as a result. While its fellows were ruthlessly felled it was spared because it marked the all-important boundary between two pieces of land.

Many of these boundary, or surveyor's, trees have kept their integrity, even after succeeding land divisions stripped them of importance. Their former public status made them common targets for the nails and staples supporting wire fences and signs. If you look closely, you may still see traces of their rusting remains where the growing wood has enveloped the wound. These slivers of wire and embedded nails are potent guardians that keep the tree from the sawmill's tender embrace. Any circular saw that has the temerity to find one in a log is sure to sustain costly damage which far outweighs the profit to be made by milling the lumber. Sawyers still refuse to have anything to do with former fence trees and they are left to grow undisturbed.

Part of a survey was the notation of such important natural features as springs, trails, and fording places. Big trees were left to serve as markers for these significant local resources.

◆ HOMESTEAD TREES ◆

When you see a pair of massive old trees towering over the surrounding forest or gracing the front yard of a modern house, stop a moment. If you look back through the years you can imagine the farmhouse that once nestled behind them. A careful walk of discovery will probably uncover other traces of past incarnations that you'd otherwise miss.

A farm cleared of all its timber was sure to keep a pair of stately shade trees out front. Often known as *husband-and-wife trees*, they were sometimes joined by plantings to commemorate each new arrival to the farm family. Although different localities favored different species for homestead trees, it is their distinctive size and placement that will catch your eye.

The farmstead also harbored trees that were nurtured because of their especially useful qualities. *Apple trees* are beacons of former settlement that you should instantly recognize. Even the meanest farm had an apple tree to provide the food and drink that were country staples. An overgrown apple tree in the woods tells you there was a farm homesite nearby. Further deduction will reveal that you are probably standing along the edge of a formerly productive field, even though the mature trees and bushes now crowding it may make that hard to imagine. Fruit trees were seldom planted in good arable land once it was cleared for crops. Instead, they were planted along the edges of the cleared area or near piles of discarded stones where they wouldn't interfere with the plow's straight furrows.

Locust trees are reliable markers of homesites in many areas, and are worth knowing as they can easily be picked out of a crowd. Wood from locusts was almost impervious to rot and made the best fence posts a farmer could wish for. The arresting and picturesque appearance of the locust tree also made it ideal for roadside or front yard planting.

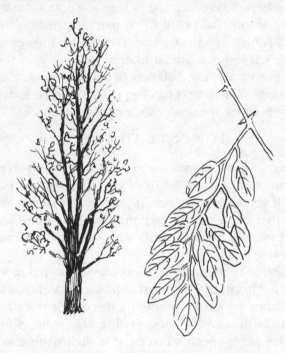

Although your main interest in trees concerns those exceptional specimens that survived from former eras, there are times when the commonplace is equally informative. Without straining your botanical acumen you can notice when all the trees in a definable area are of the same size. This information can give you a rough estimate of the fairly recent or long passed date when the field was pulled out of cultivation and abandoned to forest takeover, helping direct your further inquiries.

◆ OTHER PLANT MESSENGERS ◆

Old homesites and farms whose structures have vanished often can be spotted by their domestic plantings. Long-abandoned flowering bushes, vegetable patches, and herb gardens that once flourished close to the kitchen door may still hold their own in the undergrowth.

Asparagus and *rhubarb* are particularly hardy and well-known survivors. Many of the stands of wild asparagus stalked so avidly by springtime gourmets are unrecognized descendants of a carefully tended garden plot.

Many old farmsteads with few decorative touches still had a scattering of flowering plants to relieve the harshness of their workaday existence. Stunted *lilac* bushes and struggling clumps of *day lilies* or *daffodils* can be the signs of abandoned dreams which draw you to a former homesite.

In vast parts of the country the shortage of wood in the late nineteenth century, or simply the land's natural barrenness, presented the farmer with a pressing and unsettling problem. Adequate fencing was an essential part of successful farming, and a substitute for suddenly expensive wood had to be found. Two hedging plants served admirably until barbed wire was universally accepted. The remnants of *osage orange* and *cherokee rose* hedgerows can instantly transport you to the time of that earlier era's dilemma, and its inventive solution. (See Chapter 36, Fences.)

4.◆

THE MARKS OF SETTLEMENT

Patterns contained in the lay of the land may have pointed the way for settlement, but it was the often arbitrary order created by surveyors and homesteaders that charted its evolution. The outlines of farm fields, townships, and the patterns of city streets can help you to become attuned to the age and the character of local development.

Early colonial pioneers brought strong and identifiable European influences to American shores. Their division of the New World into settled land traced its lineage to medieval farming practices. The original surveys of seventeenth and eighteenth century America can still be discerned; their outlines faithfully preserved in the metes and bounds of scores of succeeding land transactions.

Spanish colonies in the Americas claimed huge portions of this country from Florida to California. *Pueblos* (towns) had building lots called *solares*, forming the habitations of the village proper. A small distance away, the all-important farming land was apportioned. Strips of arable land were called *suertes* and were laid out at right angles from the river or creek which invariably provided the settlement's water supply. Suertes were rarely cultivated in their entirety, in part because of the scarcity of water for irrigation, but also because of the peculiarity of their layout. Only one to two hundred feet in width, a suerte was commonly as long as ten or fifteen miles. The flocks of animals which belonged to all the pueblo's inhabitants were kept in a common pasture at a safe distance from the cultivated land.

The French in North America also favored long, narrow lots which stretched inland from the river or roadside. That layout was eminently suitable for small-scale plowing with a single team since fewer turns had to be negotiated. The French legacy is especially visible in the parishes of Louisiana.

Dutch colonists in New York followed a less orderly pattern of settlement. Enormous grants called patroonships were parceled out to wealthy owners who rarely exercised very close supervision over the land. Within the far-flung borders of these estates, tenants scattered according to individual industry, date of arrival, and the natural lay of the land, to compose a somewhat disorderly network.

New England townships were predictable creations that clearly shared a close kinship. Each was roughly six miles square, its center dominated by the village proper. The dwellings and all important village meeting house fronted on a central grassy common which was used for pasturage. The surrounding township land was apportioned in lots of varying shapes and sizes according to the industry of the individual settler and the promise of the terrain.

Growing populations spawned the formation of satellite townships as New Englanders moved deeper into the unclaimed forest. As the frontier moved westward Yankee settlers took their ideas of proper town layout with them. Many midwestern towns were built facing a central village green, bearing witness to their New England heritage.

The regularity (or lack of it) of farm sizes and field patterns holds its own story for you to read. Anyone who has spent part of a cross-country plane ride with nose glued to the window has special memories of the picture revealed below. Prominent among them is undoubtedly the famous "checkerboard" of cultivation which marks huge areas of the Midwest and other portions of the country. That unmistakable sight has a lengthy history.

Land settled during America's colonial period is a testament to the vagaries of individual industry, local custom, and an irregular landscape. Square plots of precise acreage are about the only ones you won't encounter. The holdings of early settlements form a crazy quilt of oddly shaped and sized holdings that defy easy cataloging.

This haphazard acquisition of territory ill-suited a newly independent nation intent on establishing and promoting its sovereign status. The Northwest Ordinance of 1787 was the government's solution to the problem. The national survey for which it called pulled the wildly shuffled land of variable countryside into ordered forms that were a mapmaker's delight. As further westward migration saw new territory incorporated within the national boundaries, it too was brought into conformity.

Townships were defined in 6-mile squares and consisted of thirty-six sections, each of which contained 640 acres, or one square mile. Large-scale speculators dealt in full sections but most settlers aspired to the quarter sections, the basis for the ubiquitous 160-acre farm. Quarter/quarters were standard and regularly demarked pieces of property. The phrase, "He's down in the lower forty," is still used by people who little realize that this humorous explanation of absence once had a very concrete meaning. Settlers in surveyed land knew exactly where the lower forty was in any given section.

Streets run at right angles in surveyed land, and are carefully laid out to align with the North/South axis. Sixty-nine percent of the entire country falls under the "checkerboard" of the rectangular-grid survey; most of the nonconforming land lies in the early colonized East.

The implacable grid was applied just as readily to urban locales. It was the plan of most nineteenth century cities in their entirety and was used to lay out additions to developing older settlements. Its contribution to the underlying structure of any urban city can give you an important clue to use in your assessment of any urban history. Grab it. You'll need all the help that you can get.

Cities are impossibly complex creatures to down at one gulp. The density of their historical texture is so overwhelming that a retreat to a broad site overview is often the first move you will want to make.

Irregular street patterns that defy the grid are your first objectives. There's often a section of town where winding alleys, dead ends, strangely angled crossings, and a welter of odd names create a daunting labyrinth to the casual navigator. Most often this tangle is in a grimy waterfront neighborhood of warehouses and industry. When you stumble onto it, either by design or accident, you can be quite sure you are in old, pre-survey territory. A waterfall, river junction, or other natural advantage often makes the reason for the area's settlement quite clear. If that's not the case, it's time to dig a bit deeper. Did early mineral deposits attract settlers, or was it something less readily definable? The questions themselves will guide your investigations.

Idiosyncratic streets inevitably form oddly shaped blocks that don't lend themselves to efficient development. Whenever a city or town was planned, instead of evolving in a haphazard fashion, the rational outline of a blueprint is the result.

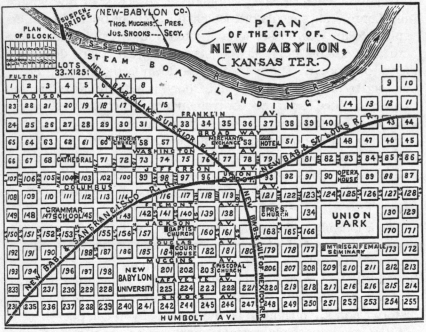

"Purely wishful thinking..."

The straightjacket of the grid is at its most overwhelming in the Midwest. Nascent cities were laid out by land speculators at every conceivably favorable location. Each mill site, landing, and river junction was sure to sport a full complement of mapped, named, and often invisible metropolises. The realities of minor obstacles such as river channels that hugged the other bank, fever-breeding swampland, and exposed flood plains rarely intruded on the speculator's dreamy calculations of possible wealth. Maps were drawn at a comfortable remove from the proposed city, while new settlers were enticed by the glowing, but profoundly empty, promises of the absentee landlord.

You are bound to see stunted and forgotten speculations surrounding every prosperous settlement. They form the outlying
neighborhoods and are skewed appendages to the central grid of
the successful site. Their traces dramatize the basic truth that every
practical pioneer acted upon: Plans and ambitions could give birth
to a settlement, but when push came to shove, survival and growth
depended on an intelligent assessment of the realities of the land.

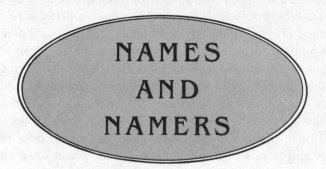

5.

NAMES
AND
NAMERS

Americans have never been stingy with names. Every natural feature, be it mountain, swamp, or bend in the road, is blessed with a name. The same location is often known by several different identities, each reflecting successive uses or waves of settlement. Joppenburgh may also be Jacob's Mount, or the Cement Hill; Route 209 can answer to the Old King's Highway or the Old Mine Road, depending on who you are talking to.

The history of a region is often set out for your inspection in the place names embellishing a modern road map, adorning wood and metal street signs, and persisting in the everyday conversational usage of local folk. The sheer number of names can be a little daunting and confounding when you first begin to notice them. Two-hundred-year-old labels are all too likely to appear alongside examples of modern suburban pretension in a confusing tangle. The Royal Grant Lane that catches your eye may be a 1976 construct—leading to Camelot Manor townhouses. As you hurry to leave the scene you may dismiss the neighboring Patent Line Road as a similar red herring and later find that you've passed up a landmark created by an eighteenth century survey.

Taken out of the context of the land and its structures, the place name is at best a mildly evocative and diverting artifact. When you view it in light of the historical patterns of settlement and development that has shaped an area, however, a street sign can point you directly into the American past.

Cultural heritages can often be read in the names defining the landscape. Indian names, liberally affixed to lakes, mountains, creeks, and other natural features, bespeak a a strong native American culture not so quickly overwhelmed by the influx of white settlers. The battlegrounds and parley sites where the two cultures clashed can be traced through markers such as *Massacre* springs, *Makepeace* creeks, and *Warrior* roads. Eventually displaced, the native Americans were hardly recompensed for their loss when the victorious settlers made free use of names like *Cherokee*, *Cayuga*, *Big Indian*, and *Choctaw* across their new homeland.

Establishing a new home in the wilderness was somehow made easier when it bore a familiar name linking it to the folks that you had left back home. *New Bostons* and *New Baltimores* celebrate the stopping points of those settlers whose roots were along the Atlantic seaboard, while *Upsalas*, *Bristols*, *Hamburgs*, *Amsterdams*, and *Gwynedds* honor European origins. Europeans came to this nation with unique skills and backgrounds which often steered them into particular areas of agriculture or industry. Transplanted place names can sometimes be clues to specific local enterprises. Wales, for instance, was a nation of extensive coal mining. Today there is a good chance that a region in this country studded with Welsh town names once had a mining economy supported by immigrant colliers.

◆ INDUSTRY AND COMMERCE
(See individual chapters on industries for additional detail.) ◆

Signposts to the sites of early industry abound in the street and place-names of the countryside and city. A road originally named for a pioneering settler might stubbornly retain its identity until encroaching civilization changed the residential or agricultural composition of the street. When a commercial or industrial enterprise opened its doors down the road from the original farmstead, a name change was often the result. The new name might have been introduced by a publicity-minded businessman willing to lubricate the palms of the county commissioners, but more often than not it was the offspring of common usage. A store built on Split Oak Road would become the natural focus of the people traveling on it. "You take the road past Brown's store until you come to the cutoff for the mill," said the local farmer to an uncertain visitor. Brown's Store Road gradually eased Split Oak Road into oblivion and, in time, the change was made official and appeared as such on maps. After Brown had closed shop and was no longer there to personally greet people, the name might undergo a further evolution and become Brown Store Road, making you scratch your head when you come across it today and wonder why a brown store would have been a notable building.

Countless forms of early enterprise were incorporated into the names dotting the American landscape. *Cooper* streets, *Lime Kiln* roads, *Tanners*villes, *Furnace* creeks, *Market* squares, to mention just a few, are well distributed across the country. You've certainly traveled on many *Mill* streets or *Old Mill* roads while going about your neighborhood or journeying through a region settled by the end of the nineteenth century. Somewhere along such a road there is sure to be the mill site that once dominated the neighborhood. And often the name of the family that ran the milling operation is also present, an added tidbit of information.

♦ **TRANSPORTATION** ♦

We're so surrounded by the incredibly engineered network of high-speed automobile interstates, parkways, freeways, and turnpikes, it is sometimes hard to slow down and let our minds travel along the older byways of the routes that shaped this nation's expansion and development.

Until the middle of the nineteenth century *waterways* were the main arteries of America, and the shoreline neighborhoods of settlements were their commercial and industrial centers. *Front* Street, or *First* Street, was the most common name for the important waterside road which abutted on the river, lake, or ocean, but growing commercial development and the occasional change in the course of water have often cost these streets their commanding vantage points. Successive spurts of fillings and construction may have left the original Front Street landlocked behind a newer *Water* Street, and an even more recent *Shoreline* Drive. On the other hand, a *Fourth* Street's present waterside perch would tell you a very different story: mute testimony to an undercut bank and catastrophic landslip at some point in the past.

Any place along the waterway that served as an entry point for commerce or travel attracted a variety of attendant activity that has left intriguing traces for your inquiring eye. You will certainly want to give locations like *Ferry* Point, Sharp's *Landing, Fording Place* Road, Elliot's *Crossing,* and *Dock* Street a careful second look.

Many times rivers and creeks were given names that told the traveler just how long he'd have to journey before coming to a spot where it was possible to cross to the other side. Ultilitarian handles like *Four Mile* Creek and *Ten Mile* River were both spawned by that prolific breeder, common usage.

For the most part, *roadways* were designed to carry local traffic. Few highways were long-distance routes in the horse-drawn age. *Post* roads were among the rare exceptions, as were the great overland routes such as the Oregon Trail and the Santa Fe Trail, which funneled thousands of hopeful emigrants westward. Potentially profitable overland routes providing timesaving shortcuts brought forth speculators willing to shoulder the expense of clearing and constructing toll roads. Any *turnpikes* you encounter on your travels that are not part of the modern, asphalt kingdom of the multilane interstate-highway system suggest a past rich in local commerce and movement.

During the last two-thirds of the nineteenth century, *railroads* dominated long-distance travel as completely as the automobile does today. Much of the comprehensive track system that brought small towns, factories, mines, and virgin territory into a network of national transportation has been dismantled for its scrap value, but its names remain to guide you along their abandoned trackbeds that were once the support of the nation's commerce. A *Depot* Street can unriddle the puzzle of an unmarked cluster of buildings, while the string of tiny towns along the axis of the Old *Spur* Highway make senses as former stops along a railroad. Watch for *Roundhouse* roads, *Railroad* avenues, *Terminal* avenues, *Water Tank* lanes, and other names suggestive of a railroading past.

◆ TOWNS AND HAMLETS ◆

They are no longer as plentiful as they were once. How many times have you wondered about the name of a road which seems to indicate the existence of a town, when there's nothing more than a straggling cluster of three or four houses? Bruceville Road runs right by your doorstep but you're certain you've never seen anything remotely resembling a Bruceville.

If you look at a late-nineteenth-century atlas of an area you know, you'll be surprised by the number of distinct localities appearing a scant half mile from one another, or perhaps indicated in a spot you know to be a particularly desolate and empty place. Terrible roads and horse-drawn conveyances made even short distances significant, and made people more aware of the special nature of their particular place on the map. These communities may have long since lost their identities, but you can be sure their siting was not capricious. There was a clear rationale. It might have been as simple as a fertile stretch of farmland that attracted a family whose descendants then spread over the adjoining fields. Perhaps it was a sulphur spring, known for its tonic effect, which sparked a sense of community identity, or a long-used mill site by the falls of the creek.

Telltale suffixes can lead you to the fascinating story behind a community's life and death. When you see a Springtown, a Dalesboro, a Roseton, a Coopersdale, a Walkersport, a Bruceville, or a Wittenburg joined to a place-name, try to uncover its unique past.

◆ CITY STREET NAMES ◆

America's astonishing westward expansion created hundreds of towns that were laid out on paper by speculators and surveyors before the first building was ever erected. Each street on the attractively displayed plat the speculator employed to lure buyers had to be named to attest to its permanence and attractiveness. Faced with all those blank spaces and in search of a persuasive and workable system, early urban planners looked to the new nation's major cities for inspiration.

Speculators with Yankee roots often turned to Boston, where streets running in both directions of the planning grid were given names. Many *State* streets, *Federal* streets, *Congress* streets, *Summer, Winter, Spring,* and *Fall* streets in cities and towns across the nation reflect the mind-set of the New England founders.

Baltimore lent its street-naming pattern to cities and towns across the Old South. Like Boston, Baltimore had names for streets running in both directions of the grid, but the names of local heroes and notables filled in the blanks on the town plat. And where local dignitaries were scarce because the land had barely been settled, the names of national heroes of the day sufficed. While *Jackson* streets are commonplace, a bit of homework will reveal others who were most esteemed at the particular time the town was formed and its streets named.

The most influential of all street-naming patterns was borrowed from Philadelphia, William Penn's carefully planned masterpiece. Cross streets were given numbers instead of names and their intersecters were baptized with a series of names which would become a litany repeated in towns and small cities across the country: *Market, Arch, Race and Vine; Chestnut, Walnut, Spruce and Pine.*

When a town father's imagination failed to produce a distinctive and acceptable name for a new settlement, heroes of the young nation were again recalled to active service. *Washingtons* and *Jeffersons,* of course, proliferated, but notables like *Fillmore* (Millard), *Tyler* (John), and *Perry* (Oliver, of the War of 1812 fame), as well as dozens of others, were also immortalized by their contemporaries. This widespread practice helps to place the approximate time of a town's founding within easy grasp.

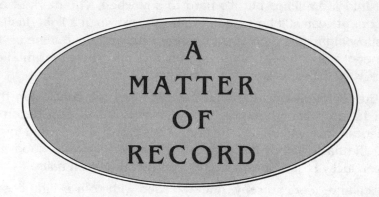

6♦

A MATTER OF RECORD

A broad knowledge of history is a wonderful thing. It lets you sketch in the landscape of the past and fill it with compellingly plausible albeit shadowy figures. The satisfaction of the conjurer grows with your knowledge as you are able to look at a building and date it with some degree of accuracy, or to mark the mill sites studding the course of a stream and notice how the landscape reflects the patterns of development. Observation, deduction, and instinct work together as you meet the challenge of walking back in time to earlier incarnations of the land.

This book, and the knowledge that inevitably percolates into your mind's clearing house from dozens of scattered sources, over the years, can let you gain a working knowledge of the language of former eras. Useful as that is, the time inevitably comes when solving the intriguing puzzle of the past demands a far greater historical fluency from you.

Specific sites are the Rosetta stones which bring history into three-dimensional living color. The old factory at the edge of town may ensnare you with its empty sluiceways, frequently amended outlines, and provocative hints of an active and varied career. Your own house is probably tugging at your curiosity if it is not a modern wonder of twentieth century standardization. When you look closely at any place that bears the marks of a former life-style, unanswered questions begin to pile up in an imposing array.

That empty house by the four corners, for instance, has intrigued you for years. Clearly it was converted from a small barn of some sort into a dwelling, but it's hard to say when. The mark of old wagon ruts can still be seen in the front yard when a light dusting of snow highlights their slight depressions, and the outline of the corner of a door leading to the hayloft is visible where the imitation brick vinyl-asbestos siding is torn away.

After carefully nosing about the premises the conclusion that you have probably found a former blacksmith's shop becomes practically overwhelming. The fireplace is clearly a converted forge, and the back wall of the attached woodshed sports a good half dozen lucky horseshoes hanging from wrought-iron nails.

Well and good, you say, quite pleased with your skillful observation, but somehow the place still tugs at you. After all, it is less than half a mile from your own house, and it must have been an important part of the neighborhood. When was it active? Who worked the bellows and turned bar iron into useful articles? Did the smith have a short and unsuccessful career, or did he make many of the iron ornaments, wheel rims, and tools still found in the yards, attics, and antique shops of the community? Why did he choose this corner for his shop, when today only an infrequent car passes by? You can satisfy your curiosity about this piece of backyard history with some concerted digging. Figurative digging, that is, as it doesn't involve turning over a single spadeful of earth.

What you need to do is documentary research, and contrary to any apprehensions you have about boredom or incomprehensible scholarly disciplines, you are actually in for some very enjoyable discoveries. All you need is a helpful guide to the several investigative tracks you can take.

◆ CIVIL RECORDS ◆

A property deed can be the opening that lets you enter the history of the blacksmith shop. If the current owner is present and amenable, you have it easy. On the first page of your soon-to-be-filled notebook, all you have to write down is the owner's name and the date the property was transferred to her. If you can't find the owner, or do and are greeted with a suspicious scowl and a quickly closed door, a trip to the town clerk is in order. Tax records for the property—be sure to take along a precise description of its location—should provide the basic information you are missing.

Armed with the owner's name and date of acquisition, head for the county clerk's office. Tell whoever is on duty that you want to see the deed for Sara Wilken's property on Sulphur Spring Road in the town of Rosendale, which last changed hands in 1961. You'll be referred to a weighty book of photostated deeds for that year, and in it will be the one you want. Turn to the proper page and you will be confronted with the standard jargon of metes and bounds, describing the property in terms of chains, nails set in the center of roads, minutes, seconds, compass readings, and the like. Skip over the whole thing and go right to the end where it will say something like, ". . . as described and purchased from Samuel Brown in liber IIX, page 474 of the county records."

You now know the name of the former owner and the location of the photostated copy of his deed. From here on it's simply a matter of backtracking from one deed to its predecessor while compiling a list of the owners' names and the dates of sale. The printed deeds of the twentieth century will often give way to the handwritten records of the nineteenth, or even the eighteenth century. You will quickly develop either a warm affection or passionate dislike for these long-forgotten county clerks—based solely on the legibility of their penmanship. If your analysis was correct, the property might be described as a blacksmith's shop. Or you could be surprised and uncover the tenancy of a wheelwright or tinsmith instead.

Tracking the sale price of the property at each turnover can also tell you something about the value of the location and the business through the years, although a deed's amount of sale need not reflect the property's real worth if it passed from one family member to another.

Because of your afternoon in the county building, the first page of your investigative diary is now beginning to take shape. Your notes will look something like this:

Location	Year	Price	Owners	Notes
Liber LXII	1961	$6,000	Sara Wilkens from Sam Brown	(house)
" LIX	1957	$5,000	Sam Brown from Richard Smith	(house)
" LV	1957	$1.00	Richard Smith from John Smith	Inheritance - check Probate
" XLII	1938	$1,500	John Smith from Owen Caradoc	(house)
" XXXVII	1918	$1,000	Owen Caradoc from Peter Wiley	Blacksmith Shop!
" XXIX	1886	$3,500	Peter Wiley from Ed Parker	Blacksmith Shop and barn
" XXVII	1878	$1.00	Ed Parker from Nathan Parker	Inheritance - check Probate
" XXIII	1864	$1.00	Nathan Parker from Caleb Sweet	Inheritance - Civil War Victim?
" XX	1854	$3,000	Caleb Sweet from John Decker	Blacksmith Shop
" XVII	1845	$500	John Decker from Jonah Hasbrouck	Raw Land - no buildings

One short session has produced a list of the property's owners and the approximate date it was converted from a blacksmith's shop to a dwelling. This may be enough information to satisfy your bump of curiosity, but more likely than not, you will find it's like a mosquito bite—the more you scratch it the more it itches. Bare facts on a page don't tell the story of the working blacksmith shop and the people who ran the forge.

Since you're already in the county office building, it makes sense for your next move to be to the room where the *probate records* are kept. Scanning the list you confirm that in 1878 and 1864 the smithy was passed to a new owner through inheritance. Ask the clerk for the wills of David Parker in 1878 and Nathaniel Parker in 1864 and you'll be directed to the appropriate records. With a little luck, you could unearth an entire listing of the smithy's contents, giving you a much better idea of the kind of business once conducted just down the street from you.

◆　　THE LIBRARY　　◆

As you begin to put your material from the county records into chronological order, the gaps are bound to strike you. Names, and isolated glimpses of the blacksmith shop's world, are certainly a major step into the past, but the characters remain shadowy and you may wish for a way to flesh them out a bit more. The next logical step, then, is to the library.

If you are in a small city or town where the library is a single building your destination is clear. In a larger city, head for the central collection, unless the local branch has been there for quite a while and has had the opportunity to amass an assortment of older books that might contain local history. Many of the books and sources you will be looking for were typically part of turn-of-the-century library collections. As far as you are concerned, the older the collection, the better.

There are several key sources that can help you to resurrect the names in your notebook. In the late 1800s it was common practice for even very small cities to have directories printed carrying residents' addresses and their occupations. By matching your deed holders' names with the directory you should be able to see how they made a living. In the case of the blacksmith shop, this isn't a stunning revelation, but the same directory also lists the occupations of other tradesmen: three carriage makers, two livery operators, a hotel owner, an assortment of teamsters, and all in the same neighborhood. Suddenly our blacksmith's location springs into focus. It was clearly a central business area along an active freight and travel route.

Commercial directories were frequently put out by railroads, canal companies, and steamship lines for the towns and hamlets along their routes. Take a look at them. There is a chance you will run across an advertisement for your blacksmith, extolling the superior quality of his work.

You might stumble upon a town history, sitting on a dimly lit library shelf, that was written for the 1876 Centennial, complete with local biographies and including one on your blacksmith and his predecessors. Be on the lookout, too, for books with dry-sounding titles like *The History of Ironworking in Jackson County*, penned by long-forgotten local authors. They can be treasure troves of anecdotes and information.

The hunt for that perfect volume that will tell you all can lead you to dusty and seldom-used library stacks. It is a journey requiring a high degree of intuitive action. The card catalog is your natural starting point, but it is useful only to steer you to the appropriate section in the library. The intricacies of subject indexing in a card catalog form an arcane (you might be tempted to call it infernal when it frustrates you for the nineteenth time) discipline. In older and smaller libraries, the cataloging can be hopelessly incomplete. Books with no official recognition miraculously appear on shelves and are only found through your specially attuned on-stack explorations. You'll find yourself getting lost in leather-bound volumes depicting the world of a century past. These books can be so beguiling that it takes real effort to remember that you are there to track down specific information.

◆ NEWSPAPERS ◆

The bound volumes of old local newspapers hold an enormously detailed picture of the everyday life of a community. The smaller the community, the longer and more intimate are the stories on local personalities, tragedies, celebrations, business transactions, and other daily concerns. A bonanza of information about the blacksmiths and their business may be buried in the yellowing pages or microfilmed reels of newspapers; unfortunately the endless detail about everything might well overshadow it. If your deed research has given you the approximate dates of an earlier owner's death, (when the deed was transferred via a will), you might be able to find an obituary, opening a page into the past. Even if you do not have a specific date, newspaper-mining can still be a useful and immensely entertaining pastime. At the very least you will get a feel for the pulse of the neighborhood over the years; and there is the very real possibility of uncovering a mother lode of articles, advertising, and the like that bring you right into the front yard of the smithy.

Collections of local newspapers can be found in several different places. Libraries often have them, in print and on microfilm. Sometimes local libraries are more apt to have the actual issues, but regional collections and college or university libraries are likely holders of microfilm copies. A visit to the office of the local newspaper is also in order. Its back files may extend back a surprising distance and include the output of earlier, long-defunct newspapers which merged or were bought out.

◆ **FAMILY RECORDS** ◆

Chapters of the Daughters of the American Revolution (DAR), local historical societies, local libraries, museums, and genealogical societies often receive centuries of family records and correspondence when people clear out their attics and garages. If you have the rare good fortune to come upon an indexed collection you might be able to find the key names that your deed research gave you. More than likely, however, you will find yourself enmeshed in this unfocussed panorama of ordinary people: letter after letter about love, death, illness, work, the weather, westward pioneering, crops, fires, in short, the minutiae of lives as they were led in the eighteenth and nineteenth centuries.

◆ **PHOTOS** ◆

Nothing quite captures the past as arrestingly as a photograph. How often have you paused to stare at the silenced hulk of an old factory building and wondered at how different the scene must have been when it was in full, earsplitting production? Or perhaps it was a river rimmed with crumbling docks and empty of all traffic except an occasional pleasure boat, which you tried to imagine thronged with ships. If you are reading this book, it is a safe bet that this kind of reverie is familiar to you. Your mental reconstruction of the past becomes increasingly solid as you integrate small clues from the landscape into your growing knowledge. Suddenly, when an old photograph falls your way, the scenes your creative intellect has erected solidify into faces, buildings, and activity.

An old photograph resurrects the immediacy of the past in the full pride of its day-to-day existence and lets you superimpose it on the often vastly changed present scene that confronts your probing eye. Vacant lots reveal their former buildings and long-vanished alleys. A photograph from the 1880s reveals that the small brick warehouse serving today as an apartment building in a residential neighborhood was once in the center of an industrial area next to a long-vanished railroad siding. The providential photograph can save you endless hours of research when a whole neighborhood, with its patterns of building and streets, is suddenly laid bare.

Obviously, photos are invaluable resources and are well worth the effort it may take to pry them from their hiding places. Head for the local college or public library's stacks and get your handy dowsing rod in action again as you browse your way through a collection of rarely disturbed old books about local personalities and history. Ask if there is a photo collection filed somewhere in the library's holdings. Often you will find yourself steered to a file cabinet bulging with unsorted, randomly labeled, and invariably fascinating images.

From the 1890s on, many of the most revealing photographs you will see are home snapshots taken with that remarkably simple invention, the Kodak camera. Local antique dealers, or even junk shops, are all too often the repositories of boxes of old photos irrevocably separated from their families. The names and identities of the people staring somberly or gaily out at you may be lost, but the land behind them is still there, even though its aspect may be dramatically altered.

Another possible source of photographs is the local senior citizen center or lunch program. Explain your interest and what you are looking for and you will probably be deluged with first- and second-hand accounts of the area's history, as well as being invited to see dozens of drawers crammed with Kodak memories.

Businesses with long tenancies on the land (look for phrases such as, "established in 1877"), have often documented their history on film. Building additions, new machinery, natural disasters, workers and their housing, shippers, and, of course, the owners' residences, were all candidates for the immortality of the camera.

◆ PEOPLE RESOURCES ◆

The enthusiasm you have for the exploration of a piece of forgotten local past comes from a deeper source than simple pride in skillful detective work. It is the promise of intimacy with people long gone that engages your interest. The search is for their workplaces, their saloons and spas, homes, farms, and streets.

It is easy to slip into an enjoyable search and find the same sense of contentment and ease that a well-written novel creates. The past is only as alive as our imaginations can rebuild it, based on the visual and written materials we can collect, and bring into play. Understanding the past life of the land and its people is an exciting and challenging game, at which you can always become more skilled. Valuable clues can be recognized with consistency once you are attuned to interpreting the traces of the physical past that still surround us. Yet, as you probe that time-shrouded local historical site, you could be totally unaware that your greatest source of revelation is sitting in a chair in the building across the street, or playing the piano at a local nursing home.

There are still many people around whose memories of this century's early decades are razor-sharp, and whose wealth of story and tradition, given them by their parents and grandparents, is massive. Their images of the land go back to the end of the horse-drawn era and antedate the widespread use of electricity. Their memories are full of detail and anecdotes and crowded with people, buildings, and activities that may have left only tantalizing traces of their passing. The stories of these witnesses can tell you more than any other research you might do.

Finding these elder residents is not that difficult. Before you begin, however, it is important to be sure of two things about yourself, your sincerity and your enthusiasm. They are precious attributes. Showing potential interviewees that you value their life stories and are eager to hear their reminiscences is the best way to evoke a rush of memory.

◆ WHERE TO LOOK ◆

Local churches and synagogues are especially good places to locate old-timers. Introduce yourself to the minister or rabbi and explain your interest. More often than not, he will lead you directly to those members of his congregation who are both accessible and full of anecdotes.

Senior citizens' groups or centers are also excellent hunting grounds. In many areas there are lunch programs for elderly residents and you should get in touch with their directors.

Local historical and genealogical societies are another source. The memories of their members are often amazingly detailed, but untapped because they see themselves as "ordinary people" with little in their histories to merit attention. You can gently disabuse them of this unworthy notion.

Don't forget to look up the directors of such civic and social organizations as the Masons, Moose, Elks, and DAR. These and similar groups probably have older citizens who were active in their communities earlier in the century and would be very willing to share their experiences with you.

As long as you project your sincere interest in these tales of everyday life, you will find most people happy to open up to you. The idea that their own memories are of historical interest to someone is novel and flattering and your search for knowledge can only benefit from their exuberance.

◆ THE INTERVIEW ◆

An enjoyable, and profitable, interview that goes where you want it to, takes a bit of preparation. First, you need to buy or borrow a cassette tape recorder to free you from the intrusive chore of taking notes. By far the best machine for this kind of work is a small portable cassette player that operates on either batteries or house current. Whenever possible, plug it into a wall socket; that way you won't have to worry about the batteries that always seem to run down just as the talk gets free ranging and fascinating. It is also crucial to use a recorder with a built-in condenser microphone. Once you push "record" on the machine you can set it on the table in front of you and forget its existence. If you have to wire a separate microphone into the recorder you could find your subject is self-conscious and talks into it instead of to you. This type of recorder is so easily forgotten that there is the temptation to sneak it into your conversation. Don't do it. Always be honest about the fact that you are taping the conversation.

Experiment with several brands of recording tape. Depending on your machine, some pick up conversation more clearly than others, and you may find the reproduction of a cheaper tape is better than that of a more expensive one.

It helps to have a clear idea about the questions you want to ask. Although there is much to be said for the unrestrained interview, you might not need forty minutes on grandchildren and food prices. You must be able to steer the talk along those paths of memory that will answer your particular questions. Doing this without being intimidating is a delicate task, but you can be firm without being authoritarian. The best way to structure your interview is to compile a series of key words and questions—which you can refer to as the talk proceeds—designed to elicit specific memories. If you want to know the history of that blacksmith shop down the street, for example, your job is fairly straightforward, and you can ask direct questions about the business and its owners.

Should your interviewee not have any distinct memories of the smithy, lead the conversation into related memories. The way the neighborhood worked and grew will tell you a great deal about the importance of the blacksmith and the type of work in which he specialized, and, who knows, along the way a specific recollection of the smithy could be unlocked. Your own list of key words and notes might look something like this:

Subject: Rose O'Connel   Born 1897 Lived in Rosendale
                                       since 1902 when
                                       father bought drugstore
                                       on corner of Elm + Canal

Ask 1. Blacksmith Shop Owners
    2. Other businesses in town
        (A) Livery stables?
        (B) Teamsters?
        (C) Hardware store?
        (D) Hotels/Inns?
        (E) Early Gas Station? When was 1st? Who had 1st cars?
    3. Prominent citizens? Many carraiges?
    4. Other people living on same corner as blacksmith
        (A) What did they do for a living?
        (B) Any still around?

◆ MAPS ◆

Treasure maps are a part of every self-respecting adventure story. When unearthed from their forgotten hiding places (often laden with a curse secured with the blood of murdered men), they lead the explorer to the untold riches of the pirate's booty, or a fabled lost mine. Of course, the maps defining the commonplace features of our workaday world are a bit less romantic, even if the amount of information they contain can actually border on the spectacular. We are all familiar with road maps that reliably chart our travels across a maze of concrete and asphalt highways, and the perplexing detail of such creations as mass transit maps has confounded many a voyager.

Most of us do not realize the extent to which our environment has been mapped. It is quite remarkable. There are maps covering geological features, population trends, insurance districts, industrial growth, waterways, railways, vegetation, farming districts, and on and on in ever-increasing detail. This cartographical bonanza is invaluable in your own forays into the past. All you need are a few nudges in the most profitable directions.

◆ IN THE COUNTRY ◆

Plat maps—precise plans or diagrams of a piece of land that show the proposed division of it—are filed deep within the county office building. Since the eighteenth century they have been a standard part of each property transaction, supplementing the verbiage of metes and bounds which describe the property's boundaries. Today's plat map shows little more than the surveyor's exact and detailed references and benchmarks, as it is limited to the confined outlines of the modern piece of property, often a single building lot. As you work your way back through the county files, however, the scope of plat maps widens. You might find an 1880 map, for instance, documenting a major subdivision of an entire neighborhood; carefully pinpointing all the individual lot holders, natural features, stores, factories, smithys, and rights-of-way. Going back still further, it is even possible that a hand-inked, idiomatically spelled first survey of the area will emerge, complete with vague placements of watercourses, Indian tracks, and a handful of pioneer homesteads.

County atlases, from the late nineteenth century, are often available and can provide clear pictures of the area's settlement, as well as its commercial life at the time of publication. Small hamlets no longer in existence except for a grouping of houses and a name on a road sign, will be carefully laid out. Embellishing the maps, will probably be some engravings of the region's leading commercial enterprises, in essence, paid advertisements.

United States Geological Survey maps are the most accessible major source of information and, in many respects, are the most fun to use. Survey maps are drawn from aerial photographs and faithfully record the look of the landscape at a given point in time. They make the patterns of settlement and industry clearly logical and reasonable. Contour lines show how the land lies—where creeks narrow and plunge down steep valleys (promising potential mill sites), and where flat bottom land undoubtedly attracted settlers. A little imagination and practice in seeing how the contour lines mirror the topography (best gotten by using a map of an area with which you are familiar) will let you "see" the land as it looked before it was settled.

Once the lay of the land comes into focus for you, the wealth of information plotted on the survey map can truly illuminate the past. Houses, barns, factories, mines, canal beds, railroad sidings, abandoned roads, and countless other specific sites stand in clearly mapped relation to one another. While many of the earliest industries around which small communities developed might have vanished before the survey map was done, the cluster of houses along a creek-side, dead-end road, where contour lines indicate a drop in elevation, might plainly suggest that a mill was once the hub of a thriving community and, in turn, prompt you to go in search of its remains.

A final note: Do not be intimidated by the symbols on survey maps. Below is a key to make their language understandable.

You can find copies of the most recent editions of the U.S. Geological Survey maps at some bookstores and most public and university libraries, in the region you are investigating. They can also be purchased directly from the government by writing the U.S. Geological Survey, Washington, D.C. 20242 and asking for an index map of your state. This will be sent, along with information on

Primary highway, hard surface		
Secondary highway, hard surface		
Light-duty road, hard or improved surface		
Unimproved road		
Trail		
Railroad: single track		
Railroad: multiple track		
Bridge		
Drawbridge		
Tunnel		
Footbridge		
Overpass—Underpass		
Power transmission line with located tower		
Landmark line (labeled as to type)	TELEPHONE	

Boundary: national			
State			
county, parish, municipio			
civil township, precinct, town, barrio			
incorporated city, village, town, hamlet			
reservation, national or state			
small park, cemetery, airport, etc.			
land grant			
Township or range line, U.S. land survey			
Section line, U.S. land survey			
Township line, not U.S. land survey			
Section line, not U.S. land survey			
Fence line or field line			
Section corner: found—indicated	+	+
Boundary monument: land grant—other	●	●

Dam with lock	
Canal with lock	
Large dam	
Small dam: masonry — earth	
Buildings (dwelling, place of employment, etc.)	
School—Church—Cemeteries	Cem
Buildings (barn, warehouse, etc.)	
Tanks; oil, water, etc. (labeled only if water)	Water Tank
Wells other than water (labeled as to type)	Oil Gas
U.S. mineral or location monument — Prospect	
Quarry — Gravel pit	
Mine shaft—Tunnel or cave entrance	
Campsite — Picnic area	
Located or landmark object—Windmill	
Exposed wreck	
Rock or coral reef	
Foreshore flat	
Rock: bare or awash	

Index contour		Intermediate contour
Supplementary cont.		Depression contours
Cut — Fill		Levee
Mine dump		Large wash
Dune area		Tailings pond
Sand area		Distorted surface
Tailings		Gravel beach
Glacier		Intermittent streams
Perennial streams		Aqueduct tunnel
Water well—Spring		Falls
Rapids		Intermittent lake
Channel		Small wash
Sounding—Depth curve		Marsh (swamp)
Dry lake bed		Land subject to controlled inundation

Horizontal control station		
Vertical control station	BM ×671	×672
Road fork — Section corner with elevation	×79	+58
Checked spot elevation		×5970
Unchecked spot elevation		×5970

Woodland		Mangrove
Submerged marsh		Scrub
Orchard		Wooded marsh
Vineyard		Bldg. omission area

Topographic map symbols of the Geological Survey; variations may be found on older maps.

ordering. You can then select the precise maps that you need.

Survey maps are available in different scales. For your purposes, the most useful series of maps is the 7½-minute series. This is the largest scale available and covers an area approximately 6½ × 9½ miles. At this scale, the details of man's effect on the land are easily seen.

◆ IN THE CITY ◆

As useful as survey maps are for interpreting the countryside, they are totally inadequate for someone exploring urban history. A densely clustered city block is certain to contain many layers of historical development which clamor for your attention. If you are examining a small city or a town, that same nineteenth century county atlas which opened rural vistas to you could have insets detailing the houses, businesses, and industry of the time. For the tracker of a large city's past, revelation comes from another source. Sanborn maps were created to satisfy the demand from insurance underwriters for explicit information about the urban structures for which they were writing policies. Block after block of a city, or town, is precisely laid out in these maps, complete with floor plans, structural materials, architectural detailing, building use, trolleys, alleys, ovens, and a host of other juicy detail.

Older incarnations of Sanborn maps (dating back to the last quarter of the nineteenth century) will probably interest you at least as much as the more recent ones, which can be ordered from the Sanborn Map Company, 629 Fifth Avenue, Pelham, N.Y. 10803. Unfortunately, the older maps are somewhat difficult to find. Try the city planner's office, the library's main branch, or the nearest major college or university. Of course there is always the Library of Congress collection in Washington, D.C., but that pilgrimage is reserved for the truly obsessed researcher, or the one fortunate enough to be close by.

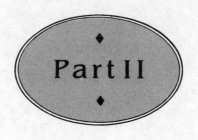

Part II

FOOTPRINTS
ACROSS
AMERICA

7 ◆

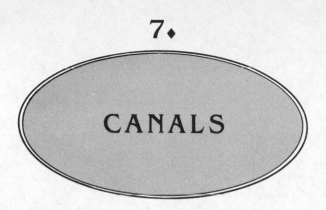

CANALS

The nineteenth century saw the rise, dominance, and total eclipse of an incredible system of man-made waterways. Canals passed so completely from the scene when railroads pushed their tracks across the country that slow-moving canalboats and placid waters quickly became romantic reminders of a rural, uncomplicated past. This dreamlike, pastoral image of the canaller's era bears slight resemblance to the dynamic history of these waterways.

To move west across a continent of dauntingly impassable forest, the white man took to the land's rivers. They were the natural roadways over which he traveled in canoes, sending back word of the interior's promise. Families and merchants followed, as did the machinery for such frontier industries as iron furnaces and gristmills so the laborious process of taming the raw land could begin.

Rivers, however, could be notoriously unobliging. They had a nasty habit of placing rapids, falls, bars, snags, and meandering channels in the path of the impatient traveler. It was particularly infuriating to deal with a malignant river's twisting, ten-mile loop, when you knew that after sweating your way through it you would be only a mile or two closer to your destination.

Despite the curses of the early river men, little was done to improve navigation inside America until shortly after the Revolutionary War. The burst of exhilaration and prosperity that swept the new nation made the creation of internal improvements a matter of commercial necessity and national pride. The formation of a network of waterways to link the former colonists in commercial and fraternal fellowship became a popular topic of discussion.

George Washington was an early supporter of the concept of a national canal system designed to open up the western wilderness to settlement and commerce. He lent his tremendous prestige to several fledgling canal companies and his lead was quickly followed by numerous monied backers. By the mid 1790s there were no less than thirty canal companies, with plans to connect man-made waterways across eight states. The construction of short canals followed, linking rivers whose courses passed close to each other, bypassing rapids, and beginning to open those navigable western avenues envisioned by Washington and his partners.

The crowning achievement of the canal-building era came between 1817 and 1825 when the "Great Enterprise" was undertaken, and the Erie Canal opened the heart of America to an astounding influx of settlers, commerce, and industry. The Erie's success galvanized both public and private companies; lengthy waterways were constructed, and the 1830s saw the country in the grip of a full-fledged canal mania. Feeder canals linked remote valleys to main routes and the future of American canals seemed secure and profitable.

The euphoria was short lived. Many of the newly constructed canals were ill-advised projects built mainly because their promoters couldn't bear the thought of being left out of the action. They were instant financial disasters for their investors and, invariably, the state governments called in to bail them out. By the late 1840s, railroads began to lay track across the country and their immediate success made the majority of American canals as outmoded as the wooden plow. Declining profits quickly weeded out those canals built in areas too underdeveloped to create a viable clientele and their abandoned towpaths often became trackbeds for the railroad companies purchasing their assets and rights-of-way. The major canals gamely limped along in spite of all obstacles, but by the turn of the century they too had largely vanished; their waters drained, beds filled, and canal towns dying.

Even though much of the canal proper may have disappeared long before your arrival on the scene, the patterns it laid on the land's settlement are there to see. Each lock was a potential townsite and the canal store, livery stable, blacksmith shop, and hotel may still stand as neighborly witnesses to the past. Industries dealing in heavy products such as bricks, pottery, ironware, glass, and stone were drawn to the canal's side by the promise of cheap shipping, and could rapidly catapult a bucolic hamlet into a thriving business center. A remote section of quiet interior farmland is about the last place you might think to look for the vestiges of active shipyards, but if you are tracking a canal you will find them, too. The passing of the canal age may have left your quarry buried under a mantle of earth and disinterest, but the impact it had on the man-made environment guarantees that its grave will not be unmarked.

◆ RANGE ◆

The eastern half of the United States in those areas settled before 1830. Concentrations in New England, the Mid-Atlantic States, Upper South, and Ohio Valley.

◆ WHERE TO LOOK ◆

Names are the easiest clues to canal history for the observant traveler to ingest. A roadsign in a sleepy rural valley pointing to the hamlet of Port Ben should immediately activate your investigative itch. There are many towns, ranging in size from tiny hamlets to densely packed suburbs, that incorporate "port," "lock," or "tow" in their names. They remain as markers to the passing of forgotten canals. Any major waterfall along a river is another location where a short canal may have been built to allow unobstructed passage for water traffic.

Roads in canal country bear names that reappear up and down their length, a bewilderment to the passerby who doesn't know their meaning. The actual bed of any former canal is probably still flanked by a *Berme* and *Towpath* Road and you are sure to stumble across roads immortalizing long-dead canal employees, names such as *Webster*'s Locks Road or *Cuddeback*'s Tow.

Railroads often bought canal rights-of-way after their competitors had bankrupted the waterway's owners. Towpaths made excellent trackbeds and canal aqueducts could be converted to train traffic with little effort or expense. The gully-like depression lying alongside the tracks in a neighborhood where you have reason to suspect a canal's existence may be much more than a simple drainage ditch. It could be the actual canal bed, now a mere servant to its successor.

If you are actively in search of canals, they are most easily found after a bit of map research in the library. The exact route of a canal was of great importance to the counties it passed through, and detailed maps were invariably included in local atlases and county histories. The county seat may well contain the actual engineering plans of the canal's construction and painstaking detail about the canal's route. (For help in learning how to ferret out this type of information see Chapter 6, A Matter of Record.)

◆ DISTINGUISHING FEATURES ◆

Many of the features of our old canals have been bulldozed, paved over, and casually obliterated in the course of day-to-day living. Your observant eye will still find many monuments to the canal's heyday as you follow its course.

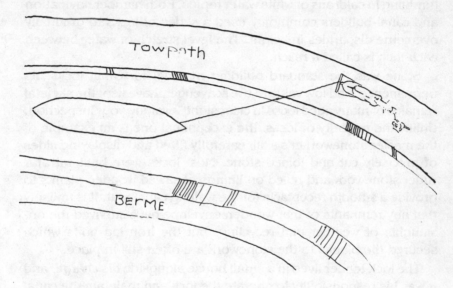

THE TOWPATH AND BERME

Old *towpaths* have stubbornly withstood the passage of time. Their surfaces, packed down by many years of slowly plodding mule, and horse teams towing canalboats, have resisted the forest's intrusion, and remain clearly defined. Much labor was exerted by canal employees working to maintain the towpath's integrity in the face of the spring freshets which periodically threatened to undermine the canal's retaining walls. A towpath break during a major storm could have disastrous results. Boats would be irresistibly swept through the gap and pile up in splintered tangles, suitable then only for firewood. If the break occured in a town, as was often the case, buildings became listing islands and the receding waters inevitably revealed muddy wastelands of destroyed property and drowned residents.

The towpath was the inviolate preserve of the horse and mule teams used to haul its traffic. Overland travelers used the paralleling roads that were frequently built on both sides of the canal. These were commonly called the *towpath* road and the *berme* road. The bank opposite the towpath was always known as the *berme* side.

LOCKS

Rivers adapt to changes in elevation by plunging in waterfalls or tumbling in caldrons of white water rapids. Both hamper navigation and canal builders commonly used a series of locks to gradually overcome disparities in height. The level stretch of water between each lock is called a *reach*.

Stone was the standard building material for canal locks. Its permanence, and low value to the scavenger, have kept the skeletal remains of many aged locks in clear sight, awaiting your inspection. Unlike the majority of locks, the exceptional one is an example of the master stoneworker's skill, carefully fitted and displaying sides of precisely cut and joined stone. Most locks were built with far ruder stonework and relied on linings of sawed wooden planks to provide a smooth receptacle for the waiting canalboat. It is unlikely that any remnants of that wooden envelope have survived the onslaughts of weather and recycling, but the iron lag bolts which secured the planks to the stonework are often still in place.

The lock tender lived in a small house alongside his charge, and it was his responsibility to operate the lock and maintain the canal reach between his post and the next lower lock. The earliest locks relied on balance beams to open and close matched pairs of paddle gates at either end of the lock, thus raising and lowering the water level. This cumbersome arrangement made it necessary for two lock tenders to be in constant attendance. By the 1850s a system of cast-iron gears and levers allowed a single man stationed in a control house straddling the lock to operate the machinery rapidly. It is possible to still find pieces of that machinery buried in the mud and trash on the lock's bottom.

Each lock had a pair of stone snubbing posts, used to secure the canalboat once it had eased its way to the lock. The friction of countless lines wrapped around the snubbing post's stone surface wore deep grooves in the resistant material. To stumble across a work-scored snubbing post still standing like an ancient sentinel by the side of the lock is to appreciate the decades of hard use which marked it.

Locks attracted buildings. By their very nature, they were stopping points which collected a captive audience of boatmen and travelers waiting for their turn, or halted by the fall of night. Most lock tenders ran a canalside store—which often doubled as their home—and enjoyed a profitable sideline selling provisions and refreshments. Taverns, hotels, and blacksmith shops often sprang up and became the nuclei of bustling canalside communities.

Because canals were avenues of transportation for both raw goods and finished products, industry naturally grew up along their towpaths. In order to accommodate this canalside activity, loading slips were built on the canal's route. Their stone-walled outlines along the dimly visible channel of the canalbed are clues that some well-established enterprise once existed there, and you might well decide to take a short investigative side trip.

If you come across a substantial rectangular stone construction, which looks for all the world like a lock leading to nowhere, and is offset by a basin where the canal widened, you have probably found a *dry dock* and are standing in a former *shipyard*. The demise of the canal's traffic made the operation of landlocked shipyards absurd, and they were immediately forgotten and abandoned, only to be reclaimed by the forest and the farmer. The remaining dry docks might confound the casual passerby, but they will alert your informed gaze: That old barn sagging alongside might just have been part of the boatbuilder's operation and still harbor traces of his work in its darkened corners and lofts.

INCLINED PLANES

Occasionally a canal builder solved the problem of moving boats from one reach to another of a markedly different elevation by building an inclined plane instead of a series of locks. Canal boats were hauled bodily out of the water and towed up wooden or cast-iron trackways by a steam engine located at the top of the ramp. No trace of the inclined plane's machinery or fittings is likely to remain, but the carefully graded rampway may still be in clear evidence along the canal route, possibly now covered with asphalt and carrying automobile traffic up the hillside.

AQUEDUCTS

Wherever the canal route crossed a river or stream of any size, it was necessary to build an aqueduct to carry the canal and its traffic above the obstruction. The massive stone piers and abutments were constructed to withstand the substantial weight of the canal and its boats and to weather the buffets of flood and ice floes from the waterways they crossed. They are probably still in place, dismissed by most passersby as the remains of an inconsequential highway bridge, when, in fact, they are the only tangible signs of a nineteenth century engineering achievement. (See Chapter 9, Bridges, for further information.)

8♦

RAILROADS

The crossing gate swings down, its warning accented by flashing red lights and a clanging bell. The freight train slowly passes by and there's nothing for you to do but settle back and watch the show. Passing in front of you is both a geography and a history lesson. Boxcars bearing the names of railroads no longer in existence, like the New York Central and Pennsylvania Railroad, are mixed into a lineup bound to include representatives from all parts of the country. Soo Line cars will be cheek-to-jowl with Southern cars, Baltimore and Ohio, Santa Fe, Rock Island, and other well-traveled veterans. The procession is a moving advertisement for a resource we take for granted—a standardized rail system which joins all parts of the country with a web of steel track. Unless your journey is inconvenienced by a freight train crossing the highway, its passage is hardly likely to register on your consciousness. Railroads are minor carriers these days and lines are being cut back every year. They have been reduced to a small part of the contemporary industrial landscape.

If you take a moment to focus your vision on the marks a century and a half of railroading have left on the land, you'll quickly see that we are literally surrounded by the skeleton of a grand past. Railroads played a crucial role in shaping the life-styles and built environment of nineteenth century America. Even if the romantic lure of an age of lovingly crafted steam locomotives fails to convert you into a bona fide railroad buff, any interest in local or regional history is bound to lead you trackside.

If your own memories stretch back to the early decades of this century you'll hardly need to be reminded of the preeminent position the train had as the carrier of the nation's goods and population. Until cars and trucks became reliable, and a network of smoothly paved roadways replaced the thank-you-ma'ams and corduroy surfaces of the horse-drawn age, almost every trip of any length was by rail. Raw materials, manufactured goods, and travelers all depended on the train. Nearly every factory, foundry, mine, warehouse, icehouse, brickyard, forge, mill, logging operation, or similar enterprise had its attendant siding. In the settled east, trackage was laid to link existing producers with established marketplaces, reflecting the economy of a country in the midst of a headlong rush into industrialization. In the West, great stretches of empty territory were opened up by railroads built for just that purpose.

Sizeable portions of this comprehensive transportation grid were abandoned as lines proved ultimately unprofitable in the face of changing economies, natural resource depletion, and the ever more formidable challenge of the trucking industry. By the time of the Second World War, many miles of empty track were targeted by scrap-recycling drives for transformation into war material, and the last forty years have seen even more ripped up for remelting.

Even when stripped of its rails, partially obliterated and largely forgotten, the old rail line can still provide crucial keys to our understanding of an area's history.

◆ RANGE ◆

The entire United States is covered by railroads, the majority of which were constructed in every state in the late nineteenth century. In the populous eastern half of the country there are traces of railroads in most counties. In the western states, areas with mining and logging industry were common locations for railroads.

◆ WHERE TO LOOK ◆

Sometimes the heading for this section might better read, "Where

Not to Look." Railroads would certainly seem to be easy to identify. Without pausing to order your thoughts, the pictures of several local stretches of track are probably flashing through your mind. Many rights-of-way have remained intact since the day they were first surveyed, and still sport their trackage even though waist-high crops of weeds tell of disuse. Why bother, you wonder, to give directions to the glaringly obvious?

The answer lies in an appreciation of the truly enormous amount of trackage that no longer exists. What's left is only a fragment from the heyday of railroading.

A short time spent with a turn-of-the-century atlas will undoubtedly show you where the major rail lines in your area ran, but actually finding the old railbeds can take some informed, on-the-spot investigation.

◆ DOWN VALLEYS ◆

The lay of the land provides your first and broadest clue to a probable trackbed. Whenever possible, engineers laying out a railroad line chose routes that followed level valley floors, thus avoiding the expense and delay of mountain construction. A quick investigation of any sizable town along the valley floor will probably uncover a *Railroad* Avenue, abandoned station, or an old right-of-way.

◆ BY INDUSTRY ◆

If you come across a cluster of elderly factory buildings planted in brick neighborliness in an outlying section of town, your search is almost sure to be rewarded. Factories, whether in town, city, or country locations, were only built where reliable transportation and/or water power were available. In order for the raw materials and finished goods to maintain a profitable two-way flow through the factory doors, by the last quarter of the nineteenth century a railroad siding was a necessity. Tracks were laid to existing plants and new industry hugged the rail lines.

◆ BY WATERWAYS ◆

Canals (see Chapter 7) predated the railroad boom by a matter of only a few decades, and their initial success in attracting industry and commerce and creating profitable marketplaces and population centers was their eventual undoing. For it was in these areas that railroads speedily appeared. Railroads offered unmatchable competition and were built by enterprising backers along routes closely paralleling the canals. A waterway's towpath and right-of-way often suffered the ultimate indignity of serving its successor when a canal company's ledgers sank under its cargo of red ink. Profitable railroads bought the assets of bankrupt canals and used their drained rights-of-way as excellent ready-made trackbeds.

Port cities on the ocean or on rivers quickly acquired a string of railroad lines which stretched inland from the docks and warehouses of the waterfront. A walk along the shoreline will surely lead you to the scene of formerly hectic railroad activity.

◆ NEAR MINING AND LOGGING ◆

Moving the weighty products of mining and logging operations was a task that short, narrow-gauge, and quickly built railroads were made for. Any old mine site probably still bears the marks of the spur that connected it to the main line of the local railroad. Ore moved out by train, and the heavy machinery used to mine and refine it was carried in on the return trip.

Tracks running into the north woods were often the only routes capable of carrying the enormous quantity of wood products demanded by a nation that had profligately gone through the wealth of its native first-growth forest. Small inland settlements strung out in a suggestively straight line in timber country are probably signposts to the presence of a railroad.

◆ DISTINGUISHING FEATURES ◆

Trackbeds are your logical starting points for a ramble into the railroading past. Even if the rails have been removed and neglect has had free rein for the last century or so, most trackbeds are still easily distinguishable from the surrounding land. The removal of topsoil and the compaction caused by years of train passage have left sharply defined areas where trees have been slow to take seed. The vegetation, too, is very different from the surrounding growth.

Horse-drawn railroads were the first versions of the rail system in this country, and in the eastern half of the country, they were used for short distances during the early part of the nineteenth century. These railroads, as well as the first steam locomotives, ran on strap rails which were wooden stringers topped with a strip of cast iron. The whole rail rested on granite blocks set into the earth at roughly one-yard intervals. These durable items might still remain firmly planted in the ground. If you chance across them you've found an ancient railroading relic. Strap rails proved a most unsatisfactory base for any heavy traffic pulled by a steam engine moving at a speed faster than a walk. The stone sleepers made the rails too rigid to give with the weight of the passing train, and they had a nasty tendency to break, and to poke up through the floorboards of the passing car. These unwelcome intruders were known as "snakeheads" by their nervous victims.

Solid metal rails were used after 1830 and they required a trackbed with a secure base that was free of frost heaves and resistant to washout. Railroad traffic was getting faster and heavier yearly, so the railroad builder carefully built a raised trackbed and topped it with a thick layer of *ballast* which had to be porous enough to allow water to seep through it. Crushed rock, gravel, cinders, or other suitable and locally available materials, were used. Tracks laid near iron furnaces used slag for ballast, while roads in the Southwest, where gravel and rock were scarce, used burnt clay and mine wastes. The ballast and raised trackbed are enduring marks for the railroad sleuth, having held their treeless course despite many decades of abandonment.

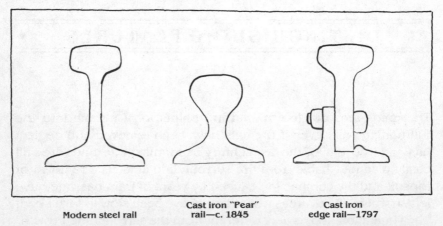

Modern steel rail   Cast iron "Pear"   Cast iron
rail—c. 1845   edge rail—1797

Rails are the characteristic marker we look for first. Before the

1870s, iron rails were used on nearly all track laid for steam lines. Iron rail is easy to identify when you lean down to take a close look at it. A smoothly curvaceous hourglass figure is the characteristic iron-rail silhouette, giving it the popular name "pear rail." The iron railhead will probably be well worn and pitted from years of use, and the whole rail will be noticeably smaller than the steel rail with which we're more familiar.

Steel became a factor in rail fabrication after the Civil War. It outlasted iron by approximately a fifteen-to-one ratio, and was increasingly used to replace worn out trackage on high-volume runs. At the end of the 1870s, the price of steel fell below that of iron for the first time. From that moment, steel was the universally laid rail. Steel rail is tall, angular, and substantial. It has probably kept its distinctive "T" shape with little sign of wear or distortion. Its strength permitted the use of heavier locomotives and larger loads than iron rails could handle.

Competition between the many rolling mills, ironworks, and steel companies eager to supply track often made the inclusion of an identifying name and date of manufacture a commonplace practice. Be sure to scan the sides of rails for these handy dating aids.

Track gauges unravel a complicated railroad history involving sectional rivalry, industrial improvisation, and frenzied expansion. If you were able to walk down a stretch of railroad in New York and then could cross the country and inspect a similar section in California, you probably wouldn't see much difference. The nationwide rail system is a seamless, uniform network which allows freight cars and travelers to be hauled to any destination without detraining. A standard gauge is responsible for this transportation uniformity. If you measure the distance between the inside edge of the railheads you'll find it is always 4' 8½" on a railroad line built since the turn of the century. This standard gauge was decreed by law in 1863, but its universal adoption came only after decades of confusion and debate.

During the first half century of railroad operation in the United States, there was little conformity to any standards. Railroads were built by men thoroughly imbued with the rationale that had ignited an earlier spate of canal construction. Railroad lines were really cheaper canals, linking one marketplace with another and opening up distinct regions for development. The railroad company stood or fell on the amount of traffic generated in its own territory, and its directors and engineers were far too engrossed in laying their own track and improving their rolling stock to worry too much about whether their line was compatible with other roads serving different marketplaces. Each line had an engineering department. Lacking a prior body of engineering solutions and models to copy, engineers wrestled with the demands of an industry that was expanding at breakneck speed. Britain had been in the railroad business for a little while, but its main contribution to the American railroad scene was the sale of early locomotives running on the 4' 8½" gauge. The northeast and Atlantic coast states retained that distance as their standard once they started manufacturing their own equipment, but in the rest of the country every aspiring engineer had his own pet idea. The result was a crazy quilt of incompatible systems that daunted efficient long-distance transport. Standard gauge could be 4'8½", 4'9", 4'10", 5'0", 5'4", 5'6", or even 6'0"—all depending on which line you were traveling. President Lincoln signed into law an act that attempted to resolve the commercially stifling gauge morass, but it took decades for a complete changeover. In the interim, broad-gauge lines often had a third or fourth rail laid on their trackbeds to permit the operation of a mixed service of standard-gauge cars linked to the wider rolling stock.

The conversion to standard gauge was an expensive undertaking as all the line's locomotives and cars, as well as the track, had to be changed over. Sometimes small rail lines found it expedient to abandon marginal branches, spurs, and sidings rather than convert them. Their rusting rails await your discovery.

Strangely enough, as standard gauge was being accepted across the country, a growing enthusiasm for *narrow-gauge* railroads was gaining momentum. Only 2'0" to 3'6" in width, narrow gauge was widely promoted during the 1870s and 1880s. The construction cost of the lightweight, narrow-gauge track was only a fraction of the standard gauge cost, and much of the elaborate trackbed preparation could be dispensed with entirely. Spurs could be run wherever a logging or mining operation needed a quick conduit to the outside world, and dismantled just as easily when they were no longer economical. Narrow-gauge lines ran throughout the country but they have left fewer signs of their passing than the more permanently constructed standard-gauge and broad-gauge railroads. If you come upon a forgotten stretch of narrow-gauge track, you'll be standing next to proof that, in that area, the last quarter of the nineteenth century was a time of hope and busy development.

Railroad ties and their dating are a handy reference point as you make your way down the old trackbed. Ties were originally shaped from the seemingly inexhaustible hardwoods of the surrounding forest. Oak was always the wood of choice but local resources put cedar, redwood, pine, chestnut, and other less frequently used woods into service. Even the most durable ties deteriorated under constant use and exposure to the elements, and periodically had to be replaced—often after less than a decade of service. As wood grew more scarce and consequently more expensive, railroad officials became close observers of tie life-spans and the comparative value of different woods and their preserving methods. From the 1880s on, track crews routinely dated each tie as it was brought in to replace a rotten oldster. The most common practice was to drive a nail whose head had been stamped with the last two numbers of the year into the top or side of the tie. If you find that a nailhead displaying "86" is the oldest tie on a section of track, and you fail to turn up any others dated later than "95," you can deduce that the line was probably abandoned sometime before World War I at the latest; service over a longer period would surely have called for massive replacements of those older ties. That bit of knowledge could help you understand the direction that towns and industries along the rail line took around that period. Perhaps the locality's ailing commercial economy made the line too unprofitable to continue. If that's the case, you can expect to find traces of an earlier boom and bust. However, if the line was closed for outside reasons emanating from a distant board of director's office, you'll want to see if the region survived the closing of this transportation artery.

Trackside structures are special rewards which can unexpectedly appear to enliven your track-walking reveries.

Section houses are regular trackside derelicts. A railroad was divided into four- to six-mile sections the upkeep of which was entrusted to a crew of maintenance workers. The section gang replaced ties and rails, renewed the trackbed's ballast, mended fences along the right-of-way, and generally made sure their section was smooth, level, and well-maintained. The section house served as the toolhouse and headquarters for the crew. Tamping bars, track jacks, picks, shovels, forks used to clean the ballast, and rail-handling equipment were stored inside. A short siding accommodated the handcars on which the work crews traveled along their alloted stretch of track.

Any siding or spur departing from the main trackbed is a signal that you might be near a vital clue to the reason for the railroad's penetration of the local neighborhood. Walking down the quiet trackbed you can feel confident that eventually you'll discover why track was built in that direction. A short stroll could easily lead you to the ruined site of an old stoneware factory, or a woolen mill, or maybe even the wreck of a grand old resort hotel which once greeted arriving passengers in high style.

Watertanks and *coal hoppers* were vital appurtenances to all railway traffic until well into the present century when the change to diesel locomotives took place.

Mileposts are regularly found wherever a rail line once ran. They informed both new engineers and train passengers of their progress to the next major depot. More often than not, your first glimpse of an old railroad milepost will probably be in a front yard where it's been placed to add a touch of decorative nostalgia to a neatly trimmed lawn. These momentos from abandoned railroads have become attractive collectibles in spite of their weight and bulkiness. Whether found in a yard or still planted along the right-of-way, mileposts can provide extremely useful information about the neighborhood and the role the railway once played there.

Each railroad had its own ideas about proper milepost construction. Many relied on the permanence of stone markers bearing carefully chiseled information. But painted wooden boards, stamped steel plates tacked on telegraph poles, and cast-iron signs were also commonly employed before the twentieth-century practice of using cast-concrete posts was universally adopted.

The milepost will bear an initial and a number, cast, painted, stamped, or chiseled on its front and back. The letter stands for the city that was either the terminal point on the line, or the next major depot. By consulting a road map you can see where the anonymous trackbed you're walking down was headed. If one side of the milepost reads "OC 36" and the other proclaims "B29," but your map doesn't reveal any cities in the appropriate positions, you might deduce that you've found a spur which ran only a short distance, and probably ended at one of your mysterious initials. Back to the road map and sure enough, Ore City shows in tiny letters—indicating a minuscule population—just about thirty-six miles due north of where you're standing. South of you along the same line is Butlerville, a fair-sized town which still appears alongside a major through rail line. It's a reasonable guess that your railroad was built solely to service Ore City in its heyday, and was abandoned when the mines shut down.

The milepost on a quiet rural lawn that states NY 96 and A53, would tell a very different story. The sleepy countryside around you was once part of the great New York City-Albany-Great Lakes transportation corridor, and consequently was linked to the commerce of the entire world. You can expect to find traces of different industries along the nearby tracks, and might also discover surprisingly cosmopolitan influences in some of the architecture and artifacts of the neighborhood. People's lives and expectations were rarely untouched when the railroad opened their worlds to the ideas and commerce of distant places. When you walk down the silent right-of-way, let the mileposts, rails, and other survivors of the past remind you of the railroad and the people whose lives were changed by its presence.

9.

BRIDGES

As you drive down the highway you rarely give a second thought to the bridges the road passes over. Most of them flash by in seconds and even the longer ones seem to serve simply as carriers of the "no passing," double white line. Probably the only bridges you can really picture as unique and distinct structures are those massive engineering accomplishments of the twentieth century which carry four-lane highways across the land's bays and rivers. Even these images are probably ones of mass and tollgates, rather than of line and construction. It's enough that we know where the span is without having to give much thought to the structure itself.

A major reason for the low recognition of bridges is today's countryside, cluttered with modern engineering marvels. Multistory buildings, interstate highways, and a host of mundane creations like giant high-tension towers are routinely accepted as ordinary structures. In this crowded landscape the commonplace bridge sinks into almost total obscurity. But among these anonymous exiles are literally thousands of historic structures which once occupied center stage in the drama of transportation and commerce in their communities.

◆ WOODEN BRIDGES ◆

Wooden bridges were the standard crossings in a land where timber was available in endless supply. Innumerable short spans were quickly erected over streams and creeks by the simple and still widely used expedient of laying a pair of large beams across the gap and mounting a roadway on top of them.

Until the Revolution, fords and ferries were the major crossings of colonial America. Land travel between the different colonies was an ordeal and the result was little commerce or communication between them. The formation of the United States directed national attention to the problem of creating reliable river crossings. The new country's leading citizens were sorely aware that internal improvements linking the former colonies in an economic and social embrace were a necessity for the nation's survival and growth. Private developers quickly undertook the construction of toll bridges across the Hudson, Delaware, Merrimack, Connecticut and Charles rivers, but their efforts were doomed to short lives. Their bridges were built low and each one relied on a lengthy series of short spans supported on closely spaced pilings to leapfrog across the water. Winter's ice and spring floods routinely caused expensive damage and interrupted traffic. The first person who could come up with a new approach to the problem was certain to be rewarded financially and acclaimed publicly. The tempting prospects were an inducement to many, and bridges of competing designs quickly spread through the land.

♦ RANGE ♦

There are about a thousand covered bridges still standing today. Nearly a quarter of them are in Pennsylvania, particularly the southern part of the state where they are still everyday stream crossings. Between them, Ohio and Indiana are host to another quarter; Vermont has nearly a hundred covered bridges within its small territory, and this density makes it the richest hunting ground for examples of the genre. New Hampshire and New York still hold on to several dozen bridges, but the other New England and Middle Atlantic states have only a sprinkling of them within their borders.

♦ WHERE TO LOOK ♦

Covered wooden bridges are extremely attractive American artifacts and the remaining specimens, often carefully preserved, are focal points of local interest. There are several books on the subject which give exact directions to their locations.

In those areas with the greatest concentration of covered bridges, be particularly alert when you're driving down small river valleys with towns and crossings that never saw their traffic increase to the point where a large modern bridge was necessary.

♦ DISTINGUISHING FEATURES ♦

Americans' answers to the problem of long spans soon began to appear over the nation's rivers. The basic knowledge about the long-span truss construction of bridges was already available in the writings of the sixteenth-century-Italian architect, Andreas Palladio.

In 1792, Timothy Palmer became the first American bridge designer to use a truss to span a wide crossing on the Merrimack River in Connecticut. *Palmer's arch truss* proved its worth even though the humped roadway was inconvenient. Subsequently he built massive bridges of carefully joined first-growth timber up and down the eastern seaboard. Palmer's 550-foot three-span Permanent Bridge at Philadelphia has the distinction of being the first covered bridge in America. Although Palmer liked to display the details of his trusswork as an advertisement for his skill, the Philadelphia Bridge Company reasoned that a covered wooden structure would be far more resistant to decay than one continually exposed to the elements. This eminently sensible addition became the standard building practice for wooden bridges erected from that time on. Today's legacy of handcrafted, coolly inviting covered bridges is the result.

The wooden-bridge-building trade boomed once Palmer's example had opened the way. Competing designs from four New England bridge builders quickly eclipsed Palmer's design and they were used nationwide. Each pattern was a product of the designer's own experience and intuitive feel of what would work. As yet there was no mathematical engineering analysis of bridge construction that was standard, so each bridge-building crew had to be made up of hands-on, practical craftsmen who learned by trial and error. Examples of these individually developed designs were built over rivers and creeks through all of the nineteenth century.

The *Burr truss arch* (1804) combined the strength of an arch with a series of multiple king posts and braces. It had a level roadway and was widely used.

The *Town Lattice truss* (1820) won wide favor because it was easily constructed from heavy planks by any competent carpenter, and was strong enough for a 200-foot span.

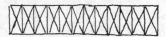

The *Long truss* (1830) was heavily promoted by its inventor and frequently used.

The *Howe truss* (1840) was signally successful as soon as it was introduced. It used wrought-iron rods secured by bolts and turnbuckles for its vertical members and had patented hardware which allowed speedy erection. Licensed bridge companies built thousands of patented Howe truss highway and railroad bridges from coast to coast.

IRON BRIDGES

Colonel Stephen Howe's discovery that iron-bridge components strengthened the structure of a wooden bridge and speeded its assembly, was a prophetic one. Bridges made entirely of iron trusses would rapidly fill the landscape.

Iron was particularly suitable for the thousands of railroad bridges being built throughout the nation. It was easily bolted and pinned together by a moderately skilled work crew, and it could be shipped directly to the construction site on flatcars loaded right at the forge and foundry. Iron bridges needed neither roofs nor walls to survive, and they were fireproof. These were major considerations when their traffic consisted of steam locomotives belching clouds of smoke and burning cinders from their stacks.

Iron also found great favor with highway-bridge contractors because of its great strength and the ease with which it could be used in construction. Cast iron was the metal used for the earliest iron bridges; however, its brittleness and lack of give made it suitable only for certain bridge components.

After 1850, wrought iron was the standard building material. It had high tensile strength and extreme toughness. The ironworking industry's explosive growth and technical prowess soon made wooden-bridge construction an outdated rural practice, reserved mainly for temporary structures which had to be put up quickly at low cost. Wrought iron was used until the 1880s when steel displaced it as America's principal building material.

◆ RANGE ◆

Iron bridges were erected everywhere the expanding transportation network created by the railroads reached. This meant most of the country. The majority of older specimens are found in the long-settled regions of the eastern half of the nation, but old iron bridges were often dismantled and shipped to new locations when they were replaced by newer and larger constructions.

◆ WHERE TO LOOK ◆

The roads you travel every day are as fine a place as any to begin your explorations. Durable old bridges surface in unexpectedly visible locations where, for years, they've simply been ignored except for routine maintenance. Some places are likelier than others, of course. You'll rarely look for nineteenth-century bridgework in a newly subdivided area, or supporting a modern limited-access highway.

Backcountry roads are places where old bridges often turn up because the minimal traffic hardly merits the enormous cost of building a modern replacement. The bridge you discover may be resting in its quiet location because of an odyssey that saw it moved from its original proud location in the center of an 1850s city. When increased traffic and heavier loads proved the original bridges inadequate for their urban locations, they were dismantled and sold to the highest bidders once replacements had been built. Used bridges were certainly cheaper than new ones, and if you weren't concerned with looks you were happy with your purchase until your own traffic outgrew it. Then, once again, the bridge was sold to someone else. This process could be repeated five or six times until an impoverished rural county highway department picked up the old veteran at a bargain price and used it for a lightly traveled highway crossing. Look at a road map and mark the county roads that cross major streams and are a little off the main travel lanes.

Locations that look as though they might have been *early industrial sites* (see Chapter 1, Waterfalls and Waterways) should be given particularly close attention. A nineteenth-century mill along the falls, which once housed a succession of manufacturing enterprises, surely had enough traffic during its prime to warrant the installation of a substantial iron bridge across the stream. If, as is so often the case, the mill fell on hard times and the area became a stagnant backwater when industry moved elsewhere, the bridge may never have been replaced by a newer structure.

Railroads, as the undisputed king of transportation during the late nineteenth century, were, in effect, the great bridge builders. The many abandoned or little-used rights-of-way crisscrossing the countryside are rich hunting grounds for early iron bridges. Every railroad company needed many structures sturdy enough to bear the weights of laden trains, and they built thousands of them. The cost of grading a track down one slope and up another when a line crossed a valley was higher in dollars and time than building a bridge over the gap. Indeed many lofty holdovers from the age of railroad prosperity remain in place long after their trackage has disappeared.

Canals ran through settled countryside and regularly passed through city and town centers; scores of bridges were needed to carry land traffic across them. You'll want to check to see if any of the original structures are still in place on the canal itself (now probably carrying a highway or railroad track). Also, watch for bridges that were moved short distances onto the back roads of towns in the surrounding area.

Large farms and country estates could often use a recycled bridge to carry an entry road across a stream or gully. Once a bridge has found a home in this private setting, the odds are good that it will be kept in place and maintained for the rest of its working life, as replacement costs have risen so dramatically.

♦ DISTINGUISHING FEATURES ♦

At first glance, iron-bridge trusses seem to present a bewildering array of types. In fact, most of them are simply variations of several basic themes. The following truss designs were the workhorses of the iron-bridge-building era and when you encounter them along an old railroad line or on a back road, they can highlight a time of tremendous industrial and commercial expansion.

Trusses could be used to support a road or trackbed in several different ways:

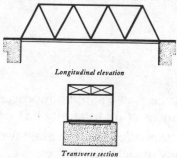

Longitudinal elevation

Transverse section

A *through truss* is the most common arrangement. As its name implies, it carries the roadway through an enclosed framework.

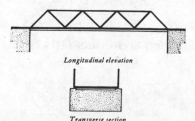

Longitudinal elevation

Transverse section

A *pony truss* was less substantial. It omitted the overhead connecting framework.

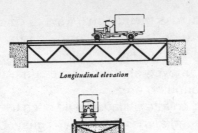

Longitudinal elevation

Transverse section

A *deck truss* carried traffic on top of its entire framework, leading to a strikingly exposed ride.

The two simplest forms of bridge trusses employ the principle that a triangular shape forms a far stronger structure than a rectangular one.

The *king-post truss* was, and still is, suitable for spans of twenty to forty feet.

The *queen post truss* was a simple improvement that could be used to bridge distances of up to eighty feet or so.

Combinations and variations of these last two were the basis for nearly all of the many truss styles that were to appear on wooden and metal bridges across America.

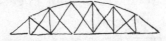

The *Whipple bowstring arch-truss* (1841) was the first and was widely used.

The *Fink truss* (1851) carried numerous railroad bridges and was often used as a deck truss.

The *Bollman truss* (1852) was another design widely used during the railroad-building boom of the late 1800s.

The simple *Pratt truss* (1844) is by far the most common of all bridge designs. It can appear in a confusing number of variations and is still the standard for most modern highway bridges.

Dating a bridge is often as simple as walking up to it and looking for a builder's plate. Most bridge contractors catered to a regional clientele and used the products of local foundries and forges. The maker's name and date of construction were prominently displayed, unless, of course, the bridge was an unlicensed infringement on a patented design.

Prior to 1890, pins and eyebolts comprised the most standard form of fastening used for iron-bridge construction. Any bridge that is riveted together is probably a later structure.

♦ ABUTMENTS AND PIERS ♦

When a bridge disappears because of a flood or because it was deliberately removed, all that remains to mark its location are its forlorn stone underpinnings. There isn't a whole lot these can tell you about the actual structure of the vanished bridge, but they can give you some general clues as to its vintage.

Concrete instantly tells you that you are looking at a site where the most recent bridge was erected after the mid-1800s. If there is no trace of stonework in the *abutments* on either shore, or on the *piers* that rose out of the water to support the bridge, probably there was never an earlier structure at that location.

Stone was the universal material used to support the timber or iron frameworks of bridges. If there are traces of a string of closely spaced piers marching across a stream, you are probably looking at a crossing that predates the widespread use of truss construction, dating from the early 1800s on.

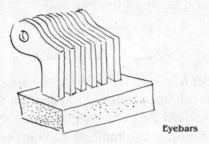

Eyebars

An abutment displaying a massed series of eyebars denotes a special artifact. *Suspension bridges* were a nineteenth-century engineering feat and rarely attempted. A handful of early pioneering designs were erected across the country in the mid-to-late 1800s and were supported by cables of twisted wire secured to the eyebars.

◆ STONE BRIDGES ◆

Stone bridges were the handiwork of early local bridge builders who had an abundance of rock to work with and wanted to build crossings capable of weathering the onslaughts of the elements. The labor in cutting and joining stone for a bridge was far greater than that needed to erect a wooden bridge. In a country with a superabundance of timber, relatively few stone bridges were constructed and most were rather rude, minor country crossings.

Bridge building was an inexact science until the middle of the nineteenth century. Contractors, faced with the need to span long distances destined to carry heavy loads, sometimes turned to stone for its strength. Canal aqueducts and railroad viaducts constructed before 1850 could be monumental stone structures indeed. The Starucca viaduct in Lanesboro, Pennsylvania has been carrying rail traffic across a valley 1,040 feet wide since its opening in 1848. Seventeen tremendous stone arches bear the weight and attest to an extraordinary expenditure of labor. Similar bridges built later in the century were nearly always wooden trestles or iron structures. Most of the stone bridges seen today bearing highway traffic or pedestrians are more recent, and were built for their appearance alone.

10◆

FERRIES

T he ferry slip was one of the busiest and most important locales of America until the twentieth century was well underway. Waterways were natural highways for transportation and commerce up and down their lengths, but they were daunting barriers to the landbound traveler intent on pursuing a straight-line journey to an interior destination. Towns grew up on both sides of a river, or they encircled a coastal harbor and faced each other across an expanse of water that was infinitely easier of passage than the tortuous journey overland. Commerce and travelers spurned the roadway and looked to the ferry for access to the neighboring areas.

The crudest ferries were found at small streams and frontier crossings. Their equipment was simple and consisted of a flat barge poled or hauled by rope across a stream that was too deep to ford comfortably. The ferry master lived at the crossing, and invariably earned additional income by using his cabin to cater to the needs of travelers, stranded by nightfall or inclement weather, for food and lodging. As the population and subsequent demand for conveyance increased, the ferry grew to more substantial proportions. A permanent slip or dock was built to accommodate a larger ferry, one too big simply to be hauled onto the bank. The ferry master's accommodations were supplemented by the opening of a regular hotel or inn, and in a short time the crossing became the nucleus of an active commercial neighborhood as business people moved in to take advantage of the steady flow of passersby.

The coming of age of the automobile doomed the ferry and its attendant neighborhoods to stagnation and decay. Highways ran in unbroken asphalt geometry across the land, facilitating nonstop travel. Massive bridges were constructed to carry land traffic across inconvenient bodies of water, and the ferry—in the time still alloted it before falling revenues forced its abandonment—became even more anachronistic.

◆ RANGE ◆

The entire country; wherever sizeable rivers, harbors, or lakes are to be found.

◆ WHERE TO LOOK ◆

The same factors that made a location attractive to an engineer selecting a site for a major bridge were often appreciated and seized upon by the early ferrymen who had no formal education or special training. It was admirably sensible to shorten a run by setting up business at a narrow point in the river or bay. The traffic-flow studies conducted by the bridge planners before construction began reflected the patterns of travel and commerce served by the existing ferries. Often ferry boats carried passengers while the skeleton of the bridge destined to replace it grew slowly overhead. Once it was complete and open to traffic, the ferry and its attendant neighborhood were doomed. Bypassed and forgotten, dwarfed by massive bridge footings, many old ferry sites are quickly sliding into oblivion.

◆ BETWEEN RIVER TOWNS ◆

Rivers are far greater barriers today than they were a century ago. That is paradoxical when we think of the twenty-four-hour, all-weather bridge crossings that defy storm, flood, and nightfall. Crossings are few, even though today's traveler thinks nothing of having to drive some fifteen or twenty miles to the nearest bridge.

When the river itself was the superhighway, and land travel was sketchy at best, there was constant traffic up and down the river. Then, too, ferries ran between most river towns that faced each other across the water. In short, the river was crisscrossed with traffic.

◆ BY RAILROAD STATIONS ◆

Ferries were vital links in the transportation grids of their day, and their locations were taken into consideration when a railroad station was built on a newly constructed line running along a watercourse. The ferry already stood where the flow of people and goods was heavy; locating a train depot close by also made the railroad accessible to the business that came from across the water. The access roads, hotels, bars, and eateries were all in place to serve the train passenger, as they had served the ferry patron, and the two modes of transportation complemented each other nicely.

◆ BY OLD HOTELS ◆

Even when a ferry has long vanished from the waterfront scene, the attendant hotel, built to profit from the captive audience of travelers awaiting conveyance, is likely to remain as a beacon for your inquiring eye. Any waterside hotel or inn, especially one which seems to be off the beaten path, is suspect. If it stands at the end of a fairly broad and lengthy street that intersects with other major roads leading to the town center or to an old U.S. highway, your suspicions are given an added boost. A hostelry tucked away in a maze of alleyways and small crooked streets is not likely to have been at the terminus of a busy ferry run. It was probably a workingman's accommodation and drew its business from sailors, boatmen, and teamsters.

◆ DISTINGUISHING FEATURES ◆

Nearly all of America's many ferries have been consigned to the realm of memory by the triumphant bridges of an all-encompassing highway system which scorns natural barriers and routes traffic and life away from the shore. Many ferries were still in operation as recently as thirty years ago, however—inheritors of businesses, and a tradition of service, that might have existed at the same site for well over a hundred years.

The ferry slip you are likely to see differs from the simple dock or landing used by the earlier ferries, which were little more than barges. A distinctive slip shape developed. It was put into universal use as specialized vessels, capable of running equally well in either direction, were built for the ferry trade. This two-faced agility substantially lessened the turnaround time needed between runs, a matter of pressing concern on the most heavily traveled lines. The ferry had to nose into its slip without undue delay at any time of the day or night, and in weather ranging from glorious to hellish.

The *spring pilings* used for ferry slips were unusually tall and formed a gently curved receptacle that guided the approaching ferry into its mooring with glovelike insistence. The height and curve of the remaining pilings are instantly recognizable and tell you that the nuzzlings of prodigious numbers of docking ferry boats had much to do with the frazzled appearance of their waterlogged timbers.

Although some terminals still stand in abandoned desolation, many became the victims of fire and vandalism and were allowed to fall to pieces long ago. It is more likely that the wide loading and unloading ramps which funneled people and vehicles onto the ferry will still be there for your inspection.

11♦

ROADS

Roads are unlikely sources of historical revelation. All of the asphalted, double-lined surfaces crisscrossing the nation in such comprehensive abundance are recent examples of the road-builder's craft. Earlier incarnations lie buried under layers of pavement or have disappeared from the landscape entirely. They yield their clues most readily to the archaeologist willing to undertake major excavation. In spite of this seeming cloak of anonymity, it is possible to distinguish important early thoroughfares and read the story of their connection with the history of their surrounding communities.

The *why* of a road's placement and the *when* of its original construction and periods of heaviest use are the essential questions to which you're seeking answers.

A passable road was a rarity in colonial America. The separate colonies existed without much intercourse or even comminication with each other except along common coastlines or navigable rivers. Game paths and Indian trails were the main arteries of land travel. While they were well-suited to hardy pedestrian traffic, they discouraged the mounted traveler and were closed to wagons and carriages. A few routes were widened and maintained as official post roads between such major cities as New York, Boston, Philadelphia and Albany, and they became early important avenues. Most other routes, however, remained barely passable tracks.

After the Revolution, the national preoccupation with internal improvements made the construction of passable roads for trade, communication, and expansion a matter of urgent concern. The push by settlers from the long-settled eastern coastline to the virgin wilderness was in full swing. The growing torrent of westward-bound travelers made the building and maintenance of key roadways a profitable undertaking.

By the year 1800, numerous *turnpike* companies had started constructing stone-surfaced toll roads across the new nation. However, during the 1830s the onslaught of canal mania sweeping the country slowed interest in overland roads and their upkeep. By the 1850s, when railroads were the key transporters of goods and people, the existing road system was allowed to settle into mud, unfrequented and unmourned. This sorry state of affairs lasted until the end of the century.

The return of public interest in passable roadways was the result of the invention of the modern bicycle. A strong lobby calling for passable highways made its presence known and stirred national interest in its cause. The invention of the auto and its later growth spawned the present highway system.

◆ RANGE ◆

Older and historically important roads are largely confined to the eastern states. They are almost exactly coincident with the dates of early regional settlement and westward expansion. Locally important roadways are, of course, found throughout the entire country.

◆ WHERE TO LOOK ◆

Watch for the oldest roads along the edges of waterways, which were the nation's major highways before the railroad's advent. River roads were nearly always beaten through the underbrush so foot traffic could return upstream.

The natural passages inland formed by *valleys* and level *moun-*

tain ridges are also likely locations of original roadways. Gauge the land and follow the path of least resistance, as you imagine an earlier pioneer might have done.

Natural features like *waterfalls, springs,* and *mineral deposits* were magnets for early settlers and generated the construction of roads to their locations.

◆ DISTINGUISHING FEATURES ◆

Many of the informative details that are part of the history of roads merit separate descriptions. (See Chapters 9, Bridges, and 12, Fords, for information.)

Roadways, by their very nature, require regular resurfacing, which completely hides their previous appearance. Only occasionally will earlier surfaces peek through a layer of asphalt or concrete, or escape modern paving entirely.

Brick roads came into widespread use in cities from the 1870s on. The earliest ones utilized regular building brick in their construction but soon a larger, more durable "paver" became the standard material. The first rural brick road was built in 1893 in Ohio, but the practice never gained widespread popularity.

Cobblestone roads were first used in fifteenth-century England and were known for their durability and extremely bumpy surfaces. There is no hard-and-fast rule for dating a cobblestone surface, but it's safe to assume that it probably preceded the widespread use of paving brick.

The most important distinguishing features you will come across as you ride down the roadway are modern signposts bearing road names. Always keep your eye trained for the revealing name which will unriddle the road's past for you. (See also Chapter 5, Names and Namers.)

◆ TURNPIKES ◆

America was plentifully supplied with natural waterways able to carry a good portion of the flood of westward emigration but they were often difficult to reach with the equipment and livestock carried by the traveler. Eager entrepreneurs formed corporations which sought to remedy the problem.

Many privately financed toll roads were built between 1800 and 1840 to cash in on the increasing movement of goods and peoples. Among them were major trunk-line turnpikes stretching for many miles and serving as main thoroughfares for travel. Their construction was a substantial undertaking and extremely expensive. Often these important roadways sported surfaces of broken stone and crushed gravel, and were hosts to regular coach and wagon services along their lengths. Branch turnpikes were local feeders and had no such presumption. Their graded, dirt surfaces allowed the reasonable passage of wheeled traffic and nothing more.

Competition from canals and railroads gutted the proud turnpike system before it could even begin to pay back its investors. The main roads, with their enormous operating costs, quickly fell into disrepair; ever muddier, washboarded, and empty of traffic. In a curious twist of fate, it was the unpretentious feeder turnpikes that often survived and profited from the change of affairs as they channeled travelers to the new railheads.

All that remains of the privately owned turnpike systems are the names printed on street signs. By the turn of the present century, the last of the private enterprises were taken over by state and local governments and incorporated into the revitalized public road network demanded by the growing bicycle lobby and the infant automobile industry.

Whenever you come across a turnpike that isn't part of the interstate system it should instantly alert you to the real possibility that many evidences of its former heyday will line the roadside. The regularly spaced appearance of substantial buildings that, incongrously, seem to be forsaken hotels in the wilderness, is explained by the turnpike's presence. So too is the abundance of manufactured artifacts, obviously brought from a distance to a seemingly isolated rural area.

♦ PLANK ROADS ♦

These former highways also remain in name only, their once highly regarded surfaces having long since returned to the soil through rot and decomposition.

In the middle of the nineteenth century, wooden roads enjoyed a brief and glorious period of national favor as *the* solution to the overland transport problem. They were built of four-inch-thick rough cut planks of oak or hemlock laid across wooden stringers. Their proponents promised they would eliminate the rutted sinkhole from the national scene.

Public enthusiasm caused thousands of miles of new wooden roadways to appear across the East and Midwest, wherever timber was available during the 1840s and 1850s. Unfortunately, it quickly became apparent that a ten-year life-span was the most that could be expected, before timbers rotted and disintegrated under the weight of heavily laden wagons. By the 1860s the seemingly limitless forests were beginning to show clear signs of serious depletion and it was evident that the regular renewal of a roadway's planks would be impossibly expensive.

Plank roads disappeared and became dirt lanes but their names were often retained and used to mark roads that were important thoroughfares in the mid-nineteenth century. Bearing that in mind, you can search for other evidences of a neighborhood's former life.

♦ U.S. HIGHWAYS ♦

Road maintenance in the eighteenth and nineteenth centuries depended on the medieval institution of statute labor. County taxes were levied in days of work instead of in cash, the theory being that the necessary upkeep of roads would then be regularly performed. In fact, the "work" gained in this fashion was nearly always minimal and poorly done. For the most part, the disastrous potholes, washboards, and quagmires endemic to the highway system remained.

In the twentieth century, the states, followed by the national government, became the overseers of important parts of the growing road network. In 1925 the familiar unified system of numbering major highways of interstate or national importance was established. Since this plan recognized the major routes that were historically important to nineteenth-century growth and travel, highway numbers are handy guideposts.

The long-traveled highway paralleling the Atlantic seaboard became U.S. 1 and important North/South roads were numbered in a westward progression ending with U.S. 101, the famous Camino Real of the padres, along the Pacific coast. The main East/West routes were distinguished as multiples of 10. U.S. 10 ran just below the Canadian border; U.S. 40 split the midsection of the country and includes the National Pike (Cumberland Road) in its route; U.S. 90 crossed the South from coast to coast.

The profusion of interstates and the unprecedented expansion of motor traffic have played a bit of havoc with this logically planned mapping, but without exception, all of the low-numbered U.S. highways follow the routes of older and important overland roads. Although later additions to the national and state highway-numbering grid tend to acknowledge existing traffic patterns, they aren't always reliable indicators of the main travel routes of the past. Today the superhighway has also eclipsed the older routes, almost as effectively as the canals and railroads once did. The cost is a faceless sterility. For a journey into the life of a region's past, you've got to slow down and roll down the old roads.

12♦

FORDS

The first water crossings in America were fording places. Early roadways acknowledged the ford's importance and angled their courses to meet it, which, in turn, helped determine the settlement patterns of the neighborhood. Fords that consistently offered good crossings were sure to turn into major travel conduits. Water depth was the first thing the traveler was interested in, but a shallow place wasn't necessarily a good ford. If the bottom was a muddy sinkhole waiting to clutch wagon wheels in its slimy embrace, few travelers were willing to attempt it. Razor-sharp rocks and swift currents also ruled out potential sites for other than occasional use.

Fords were fair-weather crossings. They had the habit of periodically disappearing under several feet of angry, rain-swollen creek, just as an impatient rider pulled up and stared longingly at the dry haven of the town across the water. Sometimes an enterprising settler built his house close by and earned a side income providing food and lodging for stranded travelers; in short order a town formed on both sides of the creek.

As soon as any substantial traffic developed around a fording place, the waterway was certain to acquire a wooden bridge which provided more reliable travel. Using the fording place, then, became a matter of choice, and many a traveler chose it to let his sweating team stop for a cooling drink on a hot summer's day.

◆ RANGE ◆

The entire country. Especially frequent in heavily settled areas with an abundance of streams, shallow and unnavigable rivers, and the like. There are fords in nearly every township in the eastern half of the country.

◆   **WHERE TO LOOK**   ◆

Look for fords next to road bridges.

The old ford periodically regained its status as the community's leading, and only, crossing when a spring freshet turned bridge timbers into splintered driftwood. Building the new bridge alongside the ford meant little interruption in travel patterns even after a disastrous flood and was a way to take advantage of the already established travel route the ford had created. The well-worn cutoff to the water's edge was always kept clear until the age when cars and massive steel and concrete bridges forever bypassed it.

Along creek banks the access to a once-used fording place might still be marked by a country lane which dead-ends at the shore and has a companion roadway visible on the opposite bank. Most of the routine upkeep on a locally important fording place was done by the town government or a private road company responsible for the roadways leading to it. A well-placed string of stepping-stones, which had to be reset annually after the spring floods, was always provided for the foot traveler. That line of heavy rock will probably have washed out of place many years ago but it may have left traces for you to discover. An abandoned section of stepping-stones would sometimes collect driftwood and silt from the creek and become the nucleus for a permanent bar or small island. If your two country lanes have a low obstruction in the creek bed between them, you might well be looking at the fording place's memorial cairn.

An important natural feature like a ford was nearly always recognized in the place-names of the surrounding communities and roadways. There are many hamlets, towns, and even cities that celebrate the old crossing with names like *Waterford*, *Glenford*, and *Woodford*.

13♦

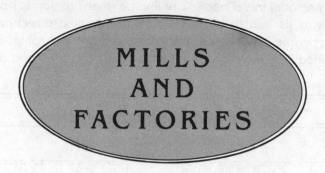

MILLS AND FACTORIES

U rban industrial sites tend to have long histories as work places. A piece of land claimed for manufacturing or heavy industry resists changes in its use with a determined and often immovable inertia. Once a massive brick factory building stands linked to the world of raw materials and marketplaces by railroads and other transportation avenues, it becomes economically attractive to a succession of tenants. In addition, industrial neighborhoods generate smoke, noise, heavy transport, and other unsightly indications of their manufacturing processes, all of which make them unlikely candidates for other uses. Old factory buildings can outlast a long string of occupants, only to end up blackened and decrepit hulks which nonetheless remain in firm possession of their identity.

In the country, small mill sites often don't maintain their obvious identifying structures with the same tenacity. Small rural mills and manufactories once dotted the settled landscape; grinding flour, making paint, sawing wood, and powering small local industry of all description. As the transportation web of railroads and canals took form in the nineteenth century, scores of communities found they could move beyond the stage of pioneering self-sufficient enclave. Mills were abandoned wholesale as outside competition broke their monopolies and growing populations, able to purchase a far wider variety of new products, passed them by. Since these minor operations were frequently built without regard to anything other than the availability of suitable waterpower, the evolving commercial and industrial America of the nineteenth century often ignored them completely and left them to rot in backwoods obscurity.

The ranks of brick-clad buildings in old industrial neighborhoods, or the solitary country ruin, may be missing from the Mobil Travel Guide but they should surely rate at least a couple of stars in your personal travel book. The lifeline of any region is bound to go back to its industrial past. The fortunes and directions that working people, businesses, and entire communities followed were determined by the types and health of their factories and mills.

◆ THE COUNTRY MILL ◆

The small country mill used to be one of the most common and important pivots of the American social and economic scene. During the first half of the nineteenth century, the number of small water-powered mills peaked at close to hundred thousand; all industriously supplying a nation of isolated rural communities with the varied necessities of life. The appearance of a rural mill that ground grain, sawed wood, or fulled cloth was often the first and strongest sign that determined settlers were ready to permanently claim the virgin wilderness. Since the irreplaceable availability of waterpower was the deciding factor in a mill's existence, it was standard practice to have several different enterprises powered by the same wheel.

A promising mill site was a prime community resource as well as an individual landowner's fortune. Local commerce and attention invariably focused on the slowly turning waterwheel.

Sawmills were everywhere. The pioneer's ongoing battle with the endless forest transformed unbelievable amounts of timber into rough-cut lumber suitable for all types of construction. The impossibility of transporting huge amounts of timber any distance when overland travel was so slow and arduous kept small local sawmills plentiful. Almost without exception, they were rather rude and insubstantial affairs which left scant physical evidence of their passing.

A country sawmill was basically a large open shed constructed of rough-cut posts and beams that housed the water-driven saw machinery. In the late 1700s and early 1800s, the sawing machines, which slowly fashioned lumber out of the trees fed into them, resembled nothing so much as oversized handsaws.

In the early 1800s, saws were often ganged together, particularly in mills near growing population centers that could support the added expense in return for a greater cutting ability.

By the middle of the century, circular buzz saws were introduced and rapidly became the standard because of their high-speed cutting ability. The once vast forests yielded supinely to the aggressive onslaught and became memories in the eastern part of the country. When coupled with the small steam engines that were mass produced in the growing industrial complex, the sawmill became totally portable. It was easily dismantled and moved when the timber nearby was exhausted.

Small water-powered sawmills in long-settled farm country tended to resist innovation and went on operating until their equipment irrevocably wore out. Their insignificant volume of business rarely made the expense of new machinery an economic alternative, and their abandoned tracks and blades can still be stumbled upon in the backwoods.

Fulling mills were also regular fixtures in the early rural countryside. Before the widespread introduction of textile mills in the nineteenth century, the universal garb of the settler was homespun. Cloth woven at home had to be shrunk and thickened in order to give it great strength and body. The *fuller* was the man who received and processed the farm family's yearly production of carefully spun cloth.

At the mill, the woven cloth was placed in long troughs of warm water called fulling stocks. Heavy oaken hammers geared to the waterwheel beat the cloth thoroughly while the addition of soap or fuller's earth completed the cleaning and processing. As anyone knows who has had the misfortune to have a prized woolen sweater slip into a pile of clothes headed for the washing machine, wool shrinks dramatically and becomes much denser when subjected to hot agitation.

When the cloth was sufficiently fulled, it was spread out to dry on tenterhooks—racks rimmed with hooked iron nails that held the cloth tight and prevented further shrinkage. The racks of finished cloth sat in front of the fuller's mill, conveniently serving as advertisements while they dried. The last step in fulling was raising the nap on the tautly spread cloth. Nature provided an admirable tool for this in the teasel, a plant whose flowering heads are filled with curved rigid bracts, making them perfectly suited for the chore.

Gristmills were the most important and long-lived members in the hierachy of country mills. A nation of small farmers depended on the services of their local miller to grind their harvests of wheat, corn, and rye into flour that could be used to feed their families throughout the year. As long as self-sufficient farmers looked to their own harvests for their sustenance, the local gristmill was assured of a busy livelihood. The continuous clamor of their grindstones, however, was checked by the urbanization of much of the nation's population by the end of the nineteenth century. The development of major centralized processors who bought enormous quantities of grain and turned them into uniformly packaged sacks of brand-name flour completed the small gristmill's eclipse.

◆ RANGE ◆

Broadly distributed throughout all areas of settlement. Small one-man operations were familiar rural fixtures and were particularly numerous in farmland in the eastern half of the country. Early mills coexist with the dates of major settlement along the eastern seaboard and important western routes.

◆ WHERE TO LOOK ◆

Water and the mill were inseparable companions until the middle of the nineteenth century when steam engines made small inroads into the industry. Any stream with a swift current, or fall of water, was a potential millsite, and was quickly marked as such by the region's first settlers. Naturally, such watercourses are your first targets for investigation. Any ponds along the stream's length, particularly if there is evidence of an artificial dam, should attract your attention immediately. The old millpond used to be a fixture of most rural communities and was instantly identifiable by any passerby. Today it has often receded far into the background of the modern landscape; silted up, drained, and largely forgotten.

The traffic the mill brought to the neighborhood's commerce often drew other businesses as well. Small towns grew around the mill building and eventually gained an identity having little to do with the mill's existence. Look for the watercourse in the town center. There, you'll often find a mill building which has long since been converted to another use.

◆ DISTINGUISHING FEATURES ◆

Waterwheels were the trademark of the rural mill. Their slowly turning bulk was an impressively graphic announcement of the millwright's skull and the wheels' power. Intact waterwheels are rare creatures these days, and are found almost exclusively in carefully tended restorations. One of the reasons for this is that most wheels of small mills were handcrafted out of wood and required constant upkeep to preserve them from the attacks of rot and the elements. When they were abandoned, decades of neglect caused them to collapse and disintegrate into shapeless ruin. The mills that operated profitably well into the nineteenth century sometimes took advantage of the burgeoning industrial community to replace their old wheels with wrought-iron creations. These borrowed heavily from the technology that made iron truss bridges a familiar sight on the landscape. If you have the fortune to discover the metal skeleton of an iron waterwheel in company with an old stone foundation, you'll be looking at a millsite which had a long run of activity.

Waterwheels fall into three main classes that are defined by the point at which the wheels receive their power. The siting peculiarities of each mill, as well as the local millwright's design preferences, determined which wheel would be put in place.

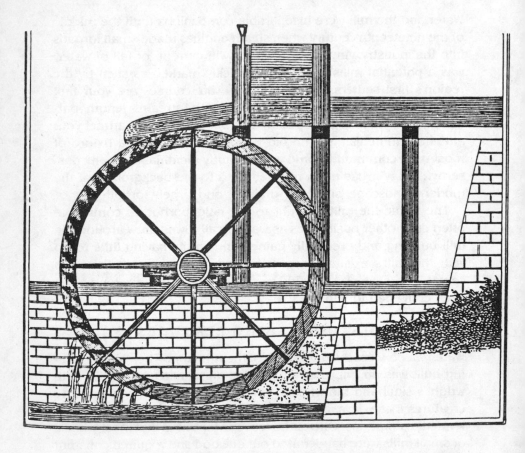

The *overshot wheel* was 75 percent efficient and most suitable for use on sluggish waterways where a dam could be built to create a high fall of water. A sluiceway carried the flow to the top of the overshot wheel and the water's weight did the work of turning.

The *breast wheel* got its drive from water channeled into it from a middle height. It was 65 percent efficient and often relied on a lock to control the flow of water to it.

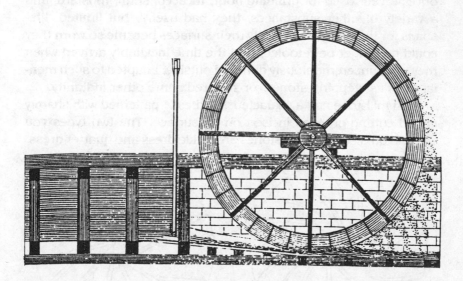

The *undershot wheel* was the least efficient, claiming only 30 percent the potential power available to it. It was common only where a fast-running stream or the racing waters below a falls provided an abundant flow of water.

For all their worth, waterwheels had several distinct disadvantages for the miller. In northern climates, ice was an enemy that could stop a wheel in its tracks and wreak havoc as it expanded with irresistible force in the wheel's unprotected sockets and joints. Waterwheels had to be enclosed and carefully tended throughout the long winter when little or no productive work could be accomplished.

The high water of spring brought with it its own problems. Rampaging freshets could hurl vast amounts of water and debris at the miller's exposed machinery, often with catastrophic results. Even the normal rise of the water level could render a mill virtually useless if the water rose high enough to drown the wheel; submerging it to the point where all its power was lost and it simply wallowed sluggishly under the weight of the high water.

During the late 1800s a solution was found in the totally submerged turbine, but it never achieved widespread favor among country millers. Most turbines spun into operation at larger industrial sites.

Millstones are indestructible traces of the thousands of mills they once served. Used for grinding flour, tocacco, snuff, mustard, and a variety of other substances, they had useful, but limited, life-spans for the miller. Eventually their surfaces became so worn they could no longer be retooled, and the time inevitably arrived when they were unceremoniously dumped outside, adapted to such menial roles as stepping stones, or suffered some other indignity.

Each millstone had a characteristic "dress," patterned with sharply edged cutting-grooves incised on its surface. The two types you will find on discarded millstones are sickle dress and quarter dress.

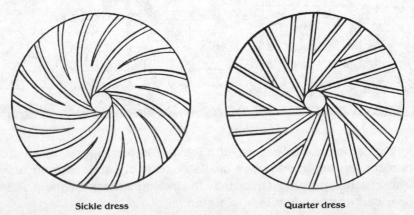

Sickle dress   Quarter dress

The debate between millers over the relative efficiency of each dress and the most useful refinements of their pattern was a hot one and never settled.

The quality of the flour produced at a mill depended largely on the quality of the stones grinding it. A good grindstone had to have an extremely hard surface to retain its cutting edges but it couldn't be too abrasive or it would powder the darker bran of the wheat and the milled flour wouldn't be white. Most country mills found local stone that was suitable for the coarse milling they did, but the miller with pretension to a quality operation bought the best product available. Although this could be a native American stone shipped from a distant quarry, for the leading millers there was only one proper course of action: Specially constructed buhr (burr) millstones were imported at great expense from France to grace their mills. Freshwater quartz quarried in northern France produced the whitest flour and provided stones that held their edge far longer than inferior products. The French stone is only found in small blocks, so a millstone, whatever its size, had to be carefully pieced together, cemented, and bound with iron bands to maintain its integrity under the strains of constant use. A buhr stone found by an old mill foundation, or embellishing the front yard of a creekside house, is a sure indicator that a quality mill once operated close by.

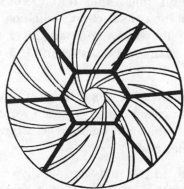

Burr Stone

Massive stone foundations were needed to underpin any small mill. The constant shaking and vibration that inevitably accompanied the milling process demanded sturdy structural support. Waterside locations, and the specter of damp rot on exposed timbers, also made stone an essential material.

Many small mills were built in locations that required an artificial augmentation of the water's natural rate of flow in order to provide sufficient power. *Milldams* built of earth, stone, or wood (and sometimes a combination of the three) were built to effectively harness the potential power of a stream that didn't have a convenient natural waterfall. By damming the flow and creating a millpond, the water of which could be released through a sluice gate at will, a more reliable and powerful flow of water could be controlled.

Races were the artificially constructed channels that directed the water to and away from the turning waterwheel or turbine. The headrace was the channel that carried water to the wheel. The tailrace was the one that returned the water to the stream once it had been used.

In addition to bringing usable water flows to the mill, races allowed the miller to place his building back from the edge of the creek where there was the potential of immediate flooding. While the solid stone underpinnings of the typical mill could easily withstand most moderate floodwaters, the threat of a massive inundation caused many sleepless nights during high-water seasons.

The flour-milling operation of the gristmill was the first fully mechanized industry to develop in the United States. From the late eighteenth century on, millwrights had access to a codified body of knowledge about the construction, maintenance, and profitable operation of gristmills. Works such as Oliver Evans' *The Young Millwright and Miller's Guide,* published in 1795, were widely known and used.

The entire operation of a properly set up mill could easily be handled by a single miller. Bags of grain were emptied into the hopper at one end while the finished, custom-ground flour was collected at the other end.

The *road* leading to the mill was always well traveled, as the miller was one of the most important members of the community. His mill was the only place where local meal could be ground into flour, and together with the local church, his was also one of the few places where the paths of farmers, normally busy with their own plots of land, would cross. Conversation and sociability were part of the mill's stock-in-trade, and a strengthened sense of community a byproduct of its existence.

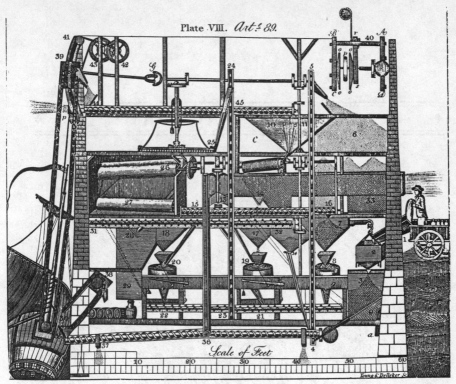

Plate VIII. *Art.º 89.*

Automatic gristmill plan, Oliver Evans, c. 1785

THE MANUFACTORY

The industrial soul of nineteenth-century America manifested itself in the legion of massive factory buildings which spewed forth the amazingly diverse and copious accoutrements of the new age. The ubiquitous small waterpowered mill supplying the immediate neighborhood was relegated to a minor place in the mosaic of commerce and expansion.

♦ RANGE ♦

Before 1850: restricted mostly to the Northeast and Middle Atlantic States; some in Southeast and in early Midwest population centers. After 1850: widespread proliferation throughout the country following the extension of railroad trackage and the creation of industrial centers across the nation.

♦ WHERE TO LOOK ♦

The earliest factories were waterpowered, often drawing substantial energy from carefully constructed power canals or major waterfalls. There were other crucial siting factors as well. A favored location along a navigable river or canal was a much more important consideration for the entrepreneur siting a large factory than it had been for the small local millowner. Quantities of raw materials and finished goods had to be easily transported to and from the factory's doors. A substantial work force was a second absolute requirement. Mills were either built to take advantage of existing settlement, or they rapidly became the hubs of thriving mill towns.

It stands to reason, then, that you head to the waterfront of a town or city in your quest for the oldest factory buildings. In most cases, you'll find that buildings from the first half of the nineteenth century stand in well-defined industrial neighborhoods which also harbor numbers of later factories. Once an industry has laid claim to an area, it rarely loses its hold. Railroads put down their tracks to factory neighborhoods in the oldest industrial regions, and transported goods and materials after the demise of water traffic, which had, in fact, prompted the early construction of the railroad.

Transport systems are your signposts for the later factories that were the progeny of industrial expansion in the late nineteenth century. Follow the railroad tracks (see also Chapter 8, Railroads) with an open eye and they will undoubtedly lead you to the factory complexes that were the base of local economies. (For specific information about key industries, consult the appropriate chapter in this work.)

✦ DISTINGUISHING FEATURES ✦

Since the utilitarian box of the factory building could house any industry dependent on ready power, it often hosted a succession of widely disparate enterprises. Today's plastics extrusion plant could be in a building that began life in the early nineteenth century as a fulling mill and later went on to house a hat maker, a piano manufacturer, a locomotive shop, even a knife maker. The only way for you to uncover the specifics about the site is to do some library hunting. (See Chapter 6, A Matter of Record.)

The history of a factory building once driven by water before being converted to other forms of power, is easily deduced from its streamside location. If you clamber down to look at its foundation you will probably find the bricked-up remains of telltale sluiceways or even the socket where the end of the massive iron gudgeon capping the millwheel's shaft rotated.

Most of the distinguishing features you can extract from the factory building hinge on details of architectural dating which are covered in Chapter 22, Architecture.

✦ THE MILL TOWN ✦

Perhaps the most eloquent statements about a factory's history are those found outside the site's gates. Mills and their work forces were inseparable. Workers in the great industrial complexes of New England, founded during the first half of the nineteenth century, lived in communities that were planned much like the prototype, Lowell, Massachusetts.

The bulk of the factory's work force was drawn from the ranks of God-fearing New England farm girls, and convenient, respectable housing was the raison d'etre of the company town. Rows of square houses with double-pitched roofs and paired doorways are still evident in every New England mill town, but today they are often sadly neglected and stripped of their repute as suitable boarding houses for young working ladies. As you wander the streets, the former hierarchy of the mill's working class becomes clear.

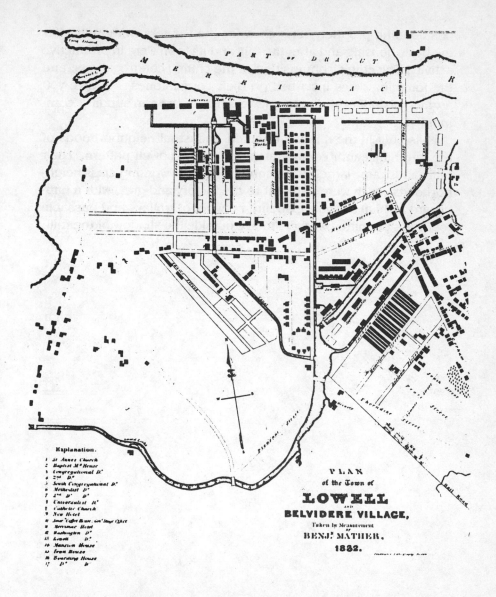

PLAN
of the Town of
LOWELL
AND
BELVIDERE VILLAGE,
Taken by Measurement
BY
BENJ. MATHER,
1832.

Explanation.

1 St. Annes Church
2 Baptist M. House
3 Congregational D.
4 2nd D.
5 South Congregational D.
6 Methodist D.
7 2nd D. D.
8 Universalist D.
9 Catholic Church
9 New Hotel
10 Post Office House, Gen'l Stage Office
11 Merrimac Hotel
12 Washington D.
13 Lowell D.
14 Mansion House
15 Iron House
16 Boarding House
17 D. D.

Near the main street and close to the actual factory, you'll find an eye-catching mansion that seems strangely out of place in the sea of smaller boarding houses. This housed the mill's agent and served as both an advertisement and a reminder of the power of the factory's influence. Second-level executives and particularly valued employees were given homes or apartments in buildings styled after the agent's mansion but reflecting a more modest sense of position and propriety. Churches for the workers were built after the basic housing and after the mill and its town were in productive activity. The ethnic composition of the church congregations, and the founding dates inscribed on their cornerstones, will give you a quick history of the probable tenancy of the surrounding community.

Mills built in the railroad-oriented, industrial neighborhoods of the late nineteenth century abandoned the Lowell pattern. Their mill hands came largely from unhomogenized working-class neighborhoods which were adjacent to the factory and grew with a haphazard fashion as the expanding network of trolleys and passable roadways permitted workers to live outside the shadow of the mill.

14.◆

BRICKYARDS AND CLAY WORKS

T he most familiar elements in our surroundings are often the ones to provide the keys to the shape of an intriguing and forgotten past. The ubiquitous brick surely ranks as one of the commonest of all building materials, mortared into place wherever the random gaze happens to fall. Bricks, as part of the European heritage known to all the early white settlers in the New World, moved across the continent as quickly as the pioneering home-steaders.

Brickmaking was a skill that was part of many a settler's home-steading repertoire. The manufacturing process was simple and followed time-honored practices which had changed little since Biblical usage. A bank of readily available clay was the major re-quirement and every pioneer was certainly able to find it close by. The clay was shoveled out and piled in a heap in the open air where it was exposed to the tempering effect of the weather for six months or so, thus making it more workable. The brickmaker then kneaded the clay by either walking on it or driving his animals back and forth across it and letting their sharp hoofs do the work for him. Once this was accomplished, a wooden form was built which was simply a rectangular frame divided into brick-sized sections. The clay was mixed with water and sand, and tamped down into the form. Then the molded blocks, known as "green" bricks, were pushed out and left in the sun to dry. No trace of moisture could remain in the green brick when it was time to fire it, as the boiling water would cause a crack or even a pulverizing explosion. When the green bricks had been dried to a turn, they were stacked up to produce a rude kiln, known as a "clamp." A hot wood fire was kindled in the middle of the clamp and it kept burning until the brickmaker was satisfied the bricks had been sufficiently fired.

Since the basic brickmaking procedures were simple and required no special equipment, individual homesteaders generally made their own bricks for that rare project needing something other than fieldstone. The homemade produce bore little resemblance to the uniform, brick-red article we instantly recognize. Each batch was a unique and never-duplicated creation. Whatever clay was handiest got mixed with sand and water to a consistency that was measured only by the hand and eye of the farmer. Each fire kindled in the clamp burned at a different temperature, depending on the wood used and the amount of stoking the homesteader felt compelled to do. When the clamp had cooled down and the finished bricks were inspected, a pile of thin, multicolored, irregularly shaped, and frequently warped objects was often the result. A common size was $1\frac{3}{4}$" × $3\frac{1}{2}$" × 7". In spite of their flaws, these home manufactures were used by settlers to build ovens, chimneys, and foundations in isolated regions not yet accessible by roads or waterways and with little commerce to speak of. As soon as an enterprising commercial brickmaker moved in and opened a brickyard, nearly everyone in the neighborhood was happy to forgo the time-consuming and uncertain job of home production, and to buy or barter for the inexpensive "real thing."

♦ THE COMMERCIAL BRICKYARD ♦

The creation of common brick, molded from local clay beds, for local building, followed close on the heels of the earliest settlement. The almost universal availability of suitable clay and the ability of a brickmaker to set up shop without purchasing any expensive equipment insured that the small brickyard would be among a region's first commercial enterprises. The same claybank also served for redware pottery and the two businesses often coexisted. (See Chapter 19, Potteries.) Bricks for items like chimneys and ovens could not be matched and the uniform product turned out by a skilled yard was preferable to the serviceable but uneven brick made on the homestead.

By 1611, there were active brick kilns in Virginia; by the end of the seventeenth century, they were found along the rest of the settled eastern coastline. As settlers moved west, their progress was paced by the brickyards. Chicago boasted the first of its many manufactories by 1802, and in 1837 Dubuque, Iowa also supported a going concern. Sutterville, California had one brickyard in 1847, but five years later the building boom, ignited by the gold rush, saw a number of businesses supplying common brick for construction.

The growth of cities, where myriads of wood-frame structures ended up in intimate, inflammable neighborliness, proved a boon to brickyard proprietors. The fear of devastating fires propelled many localities and states to pass laws mandating that all new construction taller than two stories be of either brick or stone, with slate or tile roofs. Since brick was considerably less expensive to buy and certainly easier to work with than stone, by the 1840's it became the prime building material in many of the country's urban areas. The increased demand was more than the small, traditional brickyard, which relied on hand power for kneading and molding, could handle. The brickyard became one of the earlier manufactories to profit from the technical advances of the industrial revolution. By 1840 steam presses were in place at sizeable businesses capable of gobbling up tons of raw clay and spitting out green bricks at a feverish pace. One Boston brickyard using twenty machines produced a hundred thousand bricks a day in the 1840s.

♦ RANGE ♦

The entire United States, with sites commonly located outside population centers but accessible to major transportation networks such as canals, rivers, and railroads. Particularly numerous along the Hudson Valley in New York State. Less common in the west where timber was the universally used construction material.

◆ **WHERE TO LOOK** ◆

Brickyards whose main product was red building brick rarely drew a clientele from any substantial distance. Bricks were too heavy and too cheap to incur transportation costs unless there was a canal or waterway to guarantee inexpensive shipping. Fortunately, the clay beds supplying the brickmaker's raw materials were often found along a riverbank, or revealed during a canal's construction.

Even so, it's asking a little too much of your enthusiasm to cruise aimlessly up and down the shore in search of a former brickyard. An alert eye can quickly spot a key signpost to the yard's existence. It's really fairly simple. Look for neighborhoods where there is a concentration of old brick construction. In most sections of the country brick was reserved for more substantial dwellings and commercial establishments, boasting a prosperous solidity hardly rivaled by frame construction. Around a brickyard, values were very different. The plainest and humblest homes and outbuildings are likely to show solid brick foundations and walls. A major brickyard was a large employer and supported a satellite community of workers whose lives were made financially secure by brick, and who were literally sheltered by buildings of brick.

This same reliable key also operates for small, long-forgotten, backcountry brickyards; the work force might have consisted of four or five men, and the clay bank might have been exhausted after a decade, or even less, of use. A brick building standing in incongruous stolidity in a rural area of almost complete wooden construction is very possibly the lasting advertisement and dwelling place of a brickmaker.

Clay works that manufactured items such as refractory firebrick, sewer pipe, and ornamental pressed brick, depended on shipments of suitable clay for their production. Clay for common bricks was found everywhere, but clay for firebrick and other specialized products such as stoneware (see Chapter 19, Potteries) was much rarer, and worth the cost of lengthy shipping. As a result, the entrepreneur who wanted to establish a firebrick works, for example, often staked out a site on the fringe of a major population center, and in an industrial district with ready access to railroads and shipping. The constant need for fuel to work the kilns and the accompanying threat of fire barred clay works from very populated or central locations. The factory building (brick, naturally) of the specialty brickmaker is often still standing alongside the relics of other industries with similar requirements, such as foundries and rolling mills (see Chapter 16, Ironworks).

◆ DISTINGUISHING FEATURES ◆

Oddly enough, the very works that produced as recognized a symbol of permanence and strength as the brick have vanished, leaving hardly a remnant of their structures to mark their locations. Of course, a brickyard producing common bricks didn't consist of very much. There might have been a series of mechanically stirred pits where the clay was prepared next to a small building housing the steam-driven machinery that processed raw clay into green bricks. Most of the brickyard's structure consisted of drying sheds whose sole purpose was to shield the green bricks from rain. At the end of the drying sheds there was either a series of permanent kilns where the brick was fired, or simply an open area where clamps were carefully stacked and formed their own fireboxes. If you're lucky, a string of old kilns may still mark the front of the brickyard. However, in all probability, the only structure you may be fortunate enough to find could be a towering old brick chimney used to carry off the choking smoke of the yard's work fires. Any brick outbuildings that may have been part of the operation's heyday were usually razed long ago and scavenged for their brick content. A lone chimney is an enigmatic marker, telling you only that some kind of industry was present, but keeping its own counsel about the particulars.

There is an unfailing beacon to the brickyard's past that gives you positive proof you've found the right location, so rejoice. It also tells you the name, (or at least the initials) of the brickyard. It is, of course, the eloquent *brick dump*.

Even at the largest and most mechanized brickyards, quality control was a continuing battle, and the stream of casualties was constant. A clamp of bricks never fired uniformly through its entire load, for instance. The bricks stacked farthest from the fire were often imperfectly fired and consequently earned the undignified names noggins, pluggins, and clinkers. They were fairly soft and displayed merely a tepid orange or pale cream complexion. These weaklings were suitable only for building chimneys where great strength was not required, or for putting up interior walls which were not expected to bear loads. The clamped bricks nearer the firebox assumed the familiar deep red hue and were imbued with strength to resist both outside exposure and heavy loads. The actual chamber where the fire was maintained was made of bench brick. These bricks were the hardest of the entire batch but the intense heat could leave them heavily glazed and even partially reduced to slag.

Numbers of clinkers were sure to find their way into the brick dump as unsalable and worthless trash. The vagaries of life at the brickyard were such that a large quantity of ordinary bricks and bench bricks would also be unceremoniously heaved into the ever-growing pile. Pallets that were accidentally dropped resulted in broken and worthless bricks, and periodically an imperfectly dried batch would emerge from the kiln as a distorted and motley collection of rejects.

Every major brickyard took advantage of the plastic quality of its raw material to include an effective plug for its business. The name of the brickyard was incorporated into each brick mold. Bricks became permanent advertisements for the concern. The name of the brickyard's owner confronts you thousands of times at the brick dump, just as it did the purchaser of newly fired and perfect wares. Once the bricks were laid in place the distinctive logo disappeared as it was pressed only on the top surface. But if you are ever curious about the source of the brick in a tumbledown structure, a few minutes spent knocking off old mortar will enlighten you.

The skeletal remains of the substantial transportation system that hauled weighty pallets of brick to customer's building sites, are often lastingly overlaid on the surface of the land. A small rural brickyard may still retain its access road and mounded-earth loading platforms. Any of the many brickyards that operated along canals or rivers is bound to have a well-defined road leading directly to the water's edge where the waterlogged forms of old pilings or the outline of a cut-stone slip, remain to mark the past. A railroad siding is probably in evidence if the brickyard operated in the second half of the nineteenth century and lacked access to a major waterway. The track bed's accompanying debris may give you a clue to a busy period in the brickyard's commercial life. (See Chapter 8, Railroads.)

The *claybank* is always part of the brickyard's remains. The size of the excavations can give you a valuable hint as to the prosperity and length of the yard's working career.

Another telltale key to the brickyard's importance and profitability is found in the composition of the surrounding neighborhood. A neighboring hamlet of several dozen unpretentious brick homes tells you that there was probably a sizeable work force. More often than not, there is also a single, outstanding edifice perched on a hillside and buffered by a sizeable expanse of lawn and woodland. If that building is a brick mansion, it is a safe bet the brickyard's owner was its builder and occupant. By assessing the architectural detailing (see Chapter 22, Architecture), the approximate date of the business's greatest prosperity can be fixed.

15♦

GLASSHOUSES

The first glasshouse in America was started in 1608, a scant year after the fledgling settlement at Jamestown was founded. Even though the "Jamestown" glasshouse sank into obscurity before it achieved any notable production, its very existence highlights the tremendous importance that early America placed on the glass manufactory. Glass for bottles and windows was an essential ingredient for civilization and if it couldn't be produced locally it was sure to be imported at considerable expense from Europe. This demand, coupled with the easy availability of the raw materials needed for glassmaking, inspired many entrepreneurs. Glassmaking became one of the major early industries of the United States.

Glassmaking was one of the few major industries that tenaciously held on to its medieval heritage of guild secrecy. The basic ingredients needed to make glass were simple—ample fuel for the furnace, sand, potash, and other easily acquired substances—but the proper mixture needed for an acceptable product was closely guarded information. Even more carefully hoarded was the knowledge of the skilled trade of glassblowing. It was an accomplishment learned only after a lengthy apprenticeship. Furthermore, the concentrations of glasshouses that could provide such talent were in Europe where governments were reluctant to part with skilled glassworkers, and wages were high enough to discourage the casual emigrant. Glasshouse employees had to be lured across the ocean with promises of exceptional money. Once here, they were subject to the blandishments of every competing glasshouse operator. Acquiring even the essentials for a prospective glasshouse became a worrisome and expensive proposition. And it was only one of many costly obstacles that had to be overcome.

Establishing a glasshouse, even a modest one, was a major undertaking. Crucial to the operation was the availability of enormous quantities of wood. The main furnace where the glass was made was kept in continuous blast except for the summer months and consumed mountains of fuel. As a result, the heavily forested land of the undeveloped countryside became a highly attractive location. Often an entire community had to be built in the woods, before the first bottle was blown. The glasshouse and its attendant buildings formed the core, but dwellings for a work force commonly numbering twenty-five to thirty men had to be erected as well. A sawmill was built to provide lumber and process the incoming cords of firewood; a blacksmith shop was established to forge tools and hardware; and a store was set up to sell the glasshouse's wares to the public, and to handle the goods necessary for the factory community.

The saga of New York's Ellenville Glassworks was typical. The founders of the Ellenville company had been associated with a successful glass factory in Coventry, Connecticut which had been in operation since 1813. By the late 1830s it became clear that the Coventry glasshouse was running out of wood for its furnace as the surrounding country was cleared and used for intensive cultivation. A party in search of a new location set out on a trip that took them through portions of New Jersey, New York, Pennsylvania, Delaware, and Maryland. They finally decided on Rondout, New York, a thriving Hudson River port and also the terminus for the Delaware and Hudson Canal which stretched inland one hundred miles to the coalfields of Pennsylvania. Transportation was available, and the market was strong and growing, but by the time they were ready to buy land the prices had skyrocketed. The decision was made to follow the canal inland for cheaper real estate. After a voyage of twenty-five miles they reached the burgeoning town of Ellenville and began making their purchases. First, a large plot of land for the glasshouse was acquired. Next a nearby "sand lot" that was full of the fine, clean sand needed for glassmaking, was bought. Several waterside lots, where a company canalboat slip could be constructed, and an intown lot for a glass store were then added to the roster of company property. Thousands of acres of woodlot in the surrounding countryside completed their purchases and in 1837 the glassworks was in operation.

The Ellenville Glassworks was not exceptionally large but it consumed up to 10,000 cords of wood a year and this fact meant it played a major role in populating the surrounding area. Instead of maintaining a large crew of loggers on its payroll, the company sold wooded parcels to settlers in exchange for the standing timber on the lots. As the homesteader cleared his land he brought the cut timber to the waiting glasshouse where his indebtedness was slowly erased at a princely $1.50 per delivered cord. All across the country other glasshouses were making similar impacts on the development of the countryside, as they produced the window glass and an astonishing variety of bottles that the growing population demanded.

◆ RANGE ◆

Until the middle of the nineteenth century glasshouses were concentrated in New England, the Middle Atlantic States, and a midwestern axis extending from Ohio and western Pennsylvania (with a major concentration around Pittsburgh) south to parts of Kentucky and West Virginia. In the latter part of the 1800s glasshouses were established across the entire country as the industry proliferated.

◆ WHERE TO LOOK ◆

The siting of the glasshouse was a carefully planned affair, as the Ellenville company's search through five states illustrates. The new enterprise required substantial investment and an ill-chosen location could lead to an overextended glasshouse's early demise and plunge into obscurity. What city locations lacked in the way of inexpensive property and local fuel supply, they made up for in their demand for the products. Glassworks were part of every major urban center's industrial complement and large brick factories abutted the waterside or railroad sidings that supplied them with fuel. Some may still be standing, but probably the only way you will be able to distinguish them from foundries and other industry is through the addresses in old city directories and the precise drawings in the Sanborn maps commissioned by the insurance industry. (See Chapter 6, A Matter of Record, for the how-to of tracking down this information.)

Scattered across the countryside were many other glasshouses; all carefully located to meet the demands of fuel and transportation. Most of those built prior to 1850 depended on local cordwood for their furnace fires, but as the forests shrank, any operation that hoped to remain solvent had to turn to coal or natural gas. Many late nineteenth century glasshouses were built close to the coal and gas fields of the trans-Allegheny west.

Canals and *rivers* attracted glassmakers because they provided a ready means to move the finished glassware to a broad market-place. Although local consumption was always a portion of the glasshouse's business, solvency depended on sales to a regional audience. In the latter part of the 1800s *railroad sidings* replaced the canal or river as the glasshouse's link to the consumer.

Most early glasshouses will have long disappeared by the time you reach the scene, so once again a bit of library research is your best way to narrow your search to a particular neighborhood. Once you have accomplished this, be on the lookout for surviving clusters of workers' housing, warehouses, rail spurs, and other distinguishing features that will guide you to the exact site. This will almost always be on the fringe of town or a short way into the country because the threat of fire loomed so large over glasshouses. Furnaces and ovens kept in constant blast for months at a time started many destructive fires at early glasshouses, leading, in turn, to immediate rebuilding on a larger scale, or putting an end to a marginally profitable attempt at glass manufacturing.

As with any large-scale manufactory established in the first part of the nineteenth century, the early glasshouse was usually sited to take advantage of the power provided by a reliable stream. The glassmaking process didn't depend on waterpower itself, but the sawmill that was commonly a satellite operation most certainly did.

◆ DISTINGUISHING FEATURES ◆

Furnaces were the center of every glassmaking operation and their shape and layout, even if they are only dimly visible in the masonry remains of foundations and brickwork, can tell you about the type of glass that was manufactured there. Common to every type of furnace was the massive brick smokestack that dominated the entire glasshouse. A small-to-medium sized operation with a single furnace was often surrounded with a distinctively symmetrical building. A large glasshouse might be a huge shedlike building with a roof that was pierced by the two large stacks of its furnaces and the many smaller stacks of its ovens and steam engines.

As the transformation of sand, potash, and small amounts of other ingredients into glass requires intense heat, the receptacles used to hold the charge of raw materials in the furnace were constructed with great care.

Melting pots were made of special refractory clay that could resist cracking and breaking under the high temperatures of the furnace's blast. Suitable clay was hard to find and many glasshouses imported their supplies from England and Germany. Under optimum conditions a melting pot would last only three or four months before it began to deteriorate, so the glasshouse usually had a separate *pot house* where the highly skilled work of fashioning suitable containers was done. The melting pot had three- to four-inch-thick sides and stood about four feet tall. It was often completely open at the top but for finer grades of glass, which had to be sheltered from the contamination of furnace smoke, a hooded pot was used. Fragments of discarded melting pots are frequently found in the debris of old glasshouses, and can help you to identify the site.

Melting pots

The melting pot was filled with the carefully measured batch of raw materials; a quantity of broken or scrap glass—called cullet—was also added. The ten- to twelve-hour melting and vitrification process known as founding then took place inside the furnace until the molten glass was ready to be blown.

The furnace itself was described by the number of pots it held. The brick eight-pot furnace was the most common type at a bottle glasshouse, and it turned out numberless functional and decorative containers for everything from oil to whiskey. (See Chapter 34, Bottles, for product identification and dating.) A typical bottle furnace was a domed brick structure with small work arches, about three feet from the floor and evenly spaced around its body. These arches led to the inner firing chamber.

Sheet-glass furnace floor plan, 1868
aa is the furnace
b is the annealing oven
c are the pots
d are 8' x 13' trenches

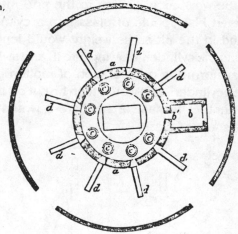

In front of each work arch stood one of the pots filled with molten glass. The glassblower dipped into this with a six- to-seven foot *iron blowpipe* and gathered a glob of the plastic material suitable for the particular bottle he intended to make. He gently blew into the end of the blowpipe to slightly balloon the hot ball of glass and then rolled it on a plate of polished iron or marble called a *maver* which was placed next to the arch's mouth to form a low table. These sheets of smooth iron may still be littering the ground of the old furnace site. This procedure shaped the glass into a conical form which was then ready to be blown. At the bottle glasshouse, the glassworker took the mavered glass on the end of his blowpipe and replaced it in the mouth of the furnace until it was very plastic. He then quickly removed it and put it into a two- or three-piece cast-iron mold, closed it and blew into the blowpipe to create a bottle. Though the whole process sounds a bit involved, a skilled workman could accomplish it in seconds. Small bottles were faster to make than large ones and a competent glassblower could create over two thousand patent-medicine bottles in a ten-hour working day.

The procedure at a factory where sheet glass for windows was the main product was similar up to the stage of mavering. At that point a distinctive furnace arrangement was required, and it may well have left traces that you can instantly identify. The sheet-glass furnace was surrounded with a series of trenches about eight feet deep and three feet wide which yawned between the glassblower and the work arch leading to the pot. After the glassblower had mavered his globule of glass into a cylinder, he deftly swung it around in the pit so its weight would lengthen it. Alternately re-heating the cylinder, blowing into it, and swinging it, he endeavored to transform the original glob of molten glass into a long, thinly walled cylinder. This would then be cut off the blowpipe and moved into another furnace arch where it would be flattened to form a large sheet of glass.

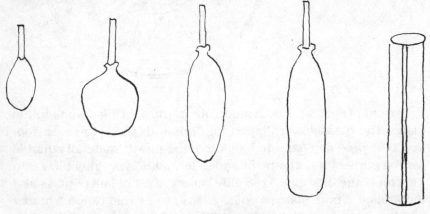

From glob to sheet

Annealing ovens were standard structures of the glassworks. Once the bottle had been molded or sheet of glass blown, it had to be brought almost to the point of melting and then allowed to cool slowly in order to temper it and give it strength. The annealing oven was always located close to the main furnace and sometimes was attached to its side. In order to keep pace with a glassblower's production, a large glasshouse could have numerous arches leading to annealing ovens.

Plate glass manufactories were a totally different operation and had more in common with the iron foundry than with the country producer of bottle glass. There were no glassblowers at the plate works. Once the pots had been founded and were ready for working, they were lifted out of the furnace with a crane and poured onto an enormous casting table which could measure 8' × 20'.

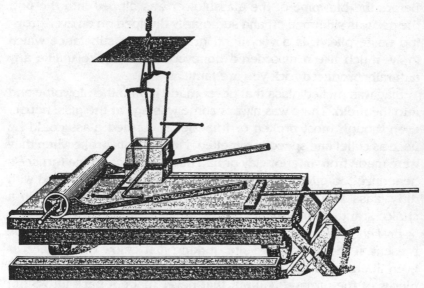

Early casting table used to make plate glass

Cast-iron rollers spread the rapidly cooling glass across the table, at which part it was pushed onto a conveyor belt of wire mesh for a short trip into an enormously long annealing oven. There it was slowly moved down to the far end and then removed when it was perfectly cool. Plate glassworks were enormous industrial operations and were most often found in the busy manufacturing districts of large cities.

Large bottles like demijohns that held up to five gallons and carboys, which were twice that size, were hand wrapped in woven willow coverings before being shipped from the glassworks. Specially trained workers, who were often German immigrants, were in charge of this important task. The glassworks frequently maintained its own *willow lot* along the nearby creek and the presence of an unusually dense and wildly overgrown stand of willows could be a revealing landmark.

Gall and *slag* abound at the glasshouse site and are easily found as you walk the ground. Exposed banks and road cuts are good places to investigate, even when nearly all other traces of the industry have vanished. Gall consists of the impurities that collected at the top of the melting pot during the ten- or twelve-hour founding period when the raw materials were transformed into molten glass. Before the blowpipe of the glassblower was dipped into the pot, the gall was skimmed off and summarily dumped on an ever-growing waste pile. It is a very light, grayish-green substance which looks much like a disordered honeycomb and quite unlike any naturally produced rock you are familiar with.

Slag was melted glass that never made it onto the blowpipe and into the mold. There was always some wastage at the glasshouse, even though most broken or imperfectly formed glass could be used as cullet and speedily remelted. Melting pots broke when they were made from inferior clay or had been exposed to the furnace's heat once too often. The result was a furnace chamber filled with dirty glass slag, to be cleaned up and thrown out along with a choice string of curses.

Broken glassware of all shapes and sizes is also bound to be present at the glasshouse site, lurking just below the surface or even littering the ground. Much of it will be broken and rejected pieces of the furnace's output that never made it back into a pot for remelting, but the customary glasshouse practice of buying scrap glass to use as cullet means that any given piece of glass you find could be the product of another glasshouse.

16♦

IRONWORKS

E nterprising Americans were quick to establish manufactories for the transformation of iron into useful items of trade and commerce. Toward the end of the seventeenth century and the beginning of the eighteenth century, most highly refined iron was imported from Europe as settlers found only low-grade bog ores were easily available to them. As soon as deposits of high-grade iron ore were discovered in abundance in the new land, companies were established to undertake the costly yet profitable task of supplying the rapidly growing population with both pig iron and a never-ending stream of tools and domestic products fashioned from it.

◆ THE FURNACE ◆

The abandoned hulk of a 150-year-old iron furnace may be the only easily spotted remnant of what was once a thriving settlement of enormous importance to a large region of developing territory. While most of the products the early settlers needed were ingeniously fashioned from the wood of the virgin forest, iron tools were indispensable for clearing the land and plowing the soil. An iron cooking pot, too, was as much a part of a pioneer's equipment as iron wheel rims, horseshoes, axes, and knives. As a homestead grew from a temporary camp to a thriving family farm, ironware was increasingly used around the house. It surfaced in hinges, latches, weather vanes, firebacks, and hollow ware of all descriptions.

As the swelling population pushed westward and opened up vast regions of land during the first third of the nineteenth century, people developed a voracious appetite for iron. Trade and commerce prospered as never before. Mills, shipyards, and tool factories clamored for high-quality iron which they could cast, hammer, and roll into thousands of guises. As the century progressed, iron became the sovereign emblem of an industrially precocious nation. Iron horses carried the vanguard of settlers across a network of iron rails secured by iron spikes. Whole buildings were prefabricated of cast iron and shipped both westward and overseas to shape the facades on thousands of main streets.

The iron furnace was where it all began. Setting up an iron furnace was an expensive and major undertaking requiring elaborate planning. First of all, workable deposits of high-grade ore were apt to be located deep in the backcountry. The common charcoal-burning furnace's insatiable hunger for fuel also meant that even a small operation had to include several thousand acres of woodlot in order to sustain the working fires. A large furnace, over the decades of its operation, could easily consume the timber from a 5-mile-square area.

The prospective ironworks entrepreneur was faced with the problem of establishing a self-sufficient and sizeable community in what was most often uncharted wilderness. Before the furnace could be built, a sawmill and gristmill had to be constructed to provide building timber and food for the workers. Of course a small blacksmith's forge had to be erected; it might also be used to smelt small quantities of ore for the on-site manufacture of tools, wheel rims, bolts, and the like. Skilled stonemasons were needed to construct the furnace and see to its repair and maintenance. They were joined by woodcutters, colliers, miners, teamsters and common laborers, all requiring housing and food. All this before even the first bar of pig iron had solidified on the furnace's casting floor. As the woodcutters cleared the surrounding land of lumber for the charcoal burners, farmers moved in and set to work supplying the community's food. The skilled workers who labored under the direction of the ironmaster to produce molten iron from raw ore increased the local population yet again. Of necessity, the ironmaster became the local storekeeper, selling the sundries needed to keep the community's members happy in their isolated industrial outpost. Invariably, he also served as the local postmaster. It's easy to see why these early settlements were commonly known as iron plantations.

The first ironworks' were often complete manufactories that produced a wide range of finished consumer goods directly on the premises. By the middle of the nineteenth century, however, when the widening network of roads, canals, and railroads brought the iron furnace into the active commerce of a rapidly industrializing nation, it became unprofitable to compete with the forges, foundries, and rolling mills located closer to the consumers. As a result, most furnaces were used simply to smelt ore into pig iron, leaving the further refinement and shaping of iron to the businesses which bought their output.

◆ RANGE ◆

Most numerous in the long-settled eastern portion of the country; with many locations in New England and the Middle Atlantic states. Fairly numerous throughout the Midwest and South; scattered in the West and Northwest. Late nineteenth century concentrations in Alabama, eastern Tennessee, and Michigan.

◆ WHERE TO LOOK ◆

It's almost impossible to track down a furnace without having done some preliminary research. There is little chance of stumbling upon one by accident unless you happen to be in one of the few areas blessed with a large concentration of stone furnace stacks. The ordinary furnace site is probably buried deep in the backcountry and concealed from sight by the thousands of acres of woodlot which once yielded fuel for its fires. The land may now be plowed farmland and the ironworks location could be hundreds of yards from the nearest road and miles from the nearest village.

An appropriate starting point for your search is the local library's nineteenth century county atlas. Evocative names like *Vesuvius* or *Etna* might well be villages that began as ironworks settlements. Or locations could be more directly pinpointed by names such as those still found in the mountains of western Virginia: *Hematite, Jordan Mines, Clifton Forge, Iron Gate, Longdale Furnace,* and *Collierstown*. Gazetteers can reveal townships where furnaces operated, and commercial directories might give you precise directions on how to reach the sites.

Nearly all furnaces shared common siting needs. Knowing those requirements makes it easier for you to find the actual location of a former plant once you have enough information to point you in the general neighborhood.

A furnace was top loaded with a charge of ore, coal, and limestone flux; the tall masonry stack was invariably erected next to a hill so a charging bridge could be built to facilitate loading. Hills and their streams were also handy when it came to securing enough water to power not only the furnace's blast machinery but the nearby gristmills and sawmills as well. Bearing this in mind, cruise around the bases of likely hills and pay special attention to the banks of any creeks or streams flowing down their sides. The remains of old roadways or railroad trackbeds should be visible. A summer tangle of vegetation makes exploration and discovery somewhat difficult. The same terrain seen under a light blanket of snow can point you directly to the furnace as the outlines of old roadbeds and building foundations magically appear.

◆ DISTINCTIVE FEATURES ◆

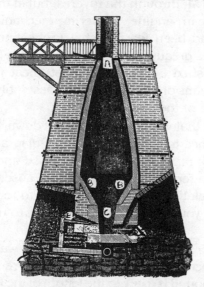

c. 1851 Charcoal
fired furnace

All furnaces were constructed on a general pattern, one designed to accomplish the relatively simple process of converting ore to molten iron. A furnace was in blast for nine or ten months at a time, barring accidents. Repair work and refurbishing were done during the winter when the furnace was blown out and production ceased.

A furnace in blast operated day and night and was continuously filled with a mixture of charcoal, iron ore, and limestone (used as a flux to promote the separation of the iron from its impurities). This charge was shoveled through a small opening called the "throat" or "trunnel head" (A on the diagram) located at the top of the stack. The bosh (B) was the tapered lower part of the furnace shaft that was directly below the shaft's widest diameter. It funneled the molten load of iron and slag into the crucible of the furnace hearth (C) and supported the tons of charge resting on its sloping shoulders. Molten iron collected in the bottom of the crucible while the lighter impurities floated to the top of the container as slag. After the slag was drawn off, the ironmaster opened the dam stone (D) and released the glowing flood of liquid iron into the molds set in a carefully prepared casting floor of damp sand. The enormous heat required to smelt a charge of ore was achieved by piping blasts of air into the bottom of the furnace through openings called tuyeres (E). The earliest furnaces relied on waterwheels to operate the outsized bellows that blasted air through the tuyeres, but in the 1800s they were replaced by steam engines powering mechanical blast machines. By 1840 it had been learned that preheating the air forced through the tuyeres greatly increased a furnace's efficiency. This was often accomplished by capturing waste heat from the furnace's own stack by means of a heat-collection assembly of cast-iron tubing placed on top of the furnace.

The actual furnace site that you manage to track down will probably bear little resemblance to the tidy schematic diagram of the previous page. The stack may be partially collapsed and its surrounding structures and attendant machinery either absent or buried under a cloak of vegetation and trash. In order to reconstruct the ironwork's fiery past, you'll need to know enough to recognize the appropriate clues.

The *slag heap* is readily located. The glassy, fused wastes created by the smelting process undoubtedly form a barren mound nearby. The size of that mound is a key to the length of the furnace's life. A small pile suggests that the furnace was blown out after a brief stretch of activity; a minor mountain indicates decades of blast.

Next, find the furnace's work arch. It is the one facing directly away from the hillside and is usually the largest arch because it provided access to the *hearth*. The smaller arches held the tuyeres that introduced the blasts to the furnace stack, and they reveal only small openings where the pipes entered.

The color of the glaze on the hearth's walls tells you if charcoal or coke was used to fuel the furnace. Wood ashes leave a white glaze and coat the interiors of most of the furnaces you are likely to discover. The black glaze on the hearth of a coke-fired furnace means you are looking at a relatively young furnace. Coke wasn't widely used for fuel until there was a nationwide railroad network that could transport the coke from the coal fields to distant inland sites. It was not until after the Civil War that numbers of ironmasters began to regard coke as a financially attractive alternative to the inordinate labor of woodcutting and charcoal making.

Directly in front of the work arch you'll find the *casting floor*. Your quarry as an investigator here is the pig, the sow, and the pig bed. This isn't really a digression on life in the barnyard. The iron-workers of a rural age called the smaller oblong chunks of iron, cast for transport to a forge or rolling mill, pigs. Naturally they dubbed the larger versions sows.

The name of the furnace was often stamped into the mold of the pig and was useful as advertising, much as bricks were that bore the name of their brickyard. The pig bed was simply that part of the casting floor where molds for pigs were pressed into the damp sand. Sometimes the outlines of the casting floor are clearly visible in the foundation work; however, often no such trace remains. The thick layer of sand that formed the floor's bed is certain to be under the overgrowth of vegetation. Examine the plants as you probe. Those growing over the casting floor will probably show the effects of their particular soil composition and be quite different from their sand-free neighbors (see Chapter 3, Plant Language).

Near the furnace body you should find, at the very least, the foundation of the large building that served as the *charcoal house*. This was where fuel was stored prior to its mixing with iron and flux. A wealth of charcoal fragments will confirm its identity, as will a well-worn path between its doorway and the charging bridge by the top of the furnace stack.

Also close by is the site of the furnace's *scrap heap* where odd pieces of iron, broken pigs, and imperfect castings were collected for later remelting. Although the main production of many furnaces was pig iron for industrial customers, articles such as stove plates or domestic hollow ware (pots, skillets, and the like) were often cast on the same floor. There's a real chance you will find a broken casting of one of the articles produced at the factory. Photograph it, if you can.

Should the only fragments of iron you unearth bear no resemblance to any product you can figure out, a hammer and a magnifying glass will help you to do some revealing on-site analysis. Iron was smelted at the furnace to produce pigs of fairly low purity. Break off a small piece of scrap and examine it under your magnifying glass. If it is soft enough to dent, dark gray, and shot full of dark specks of graphite, you are holding a piece of *#1 pig iron*. #1 was the lowest-grade metal smelted at a furnace. It had little strength but was suitable for casting into ornate stove plates and domestic hollow ware. Some furnaces never produced any finer iron and contented themselves with a limited market. If your fracture reveals a light gray iron that is free of the peppering of graphite you have a *#2 pig iron*. This was the standard, all-purpose iron used in the industry for high-quality castings of many different types.

When the ironmaster released the furnace's dam stone, # 2 pig iron was the purest product he could hope to find. As good as it was, it was totally unsuitable for the casting of heavy machine parts or structural building members. In order to achieve the requisite strength, the furnace's pigs had to be further refined to reduce their carbon and slag content. If you discover any of the following types of iron on your scrap heap, it's a definite indication that the furnace community contained a specialized subindustry of metalworkers who vied with distant foundries and forges in a marketplace which became increasingly competitive after the middle of the nineteenth century.

#3 pig iron is very light in color, and you were probably perspiring before you managed to break off a piece of it. It is very strong stuff and was used for the casting of large pieces such as structural iron beams.

#4 pig iron is almost white and also of great strength. It was used only to cast the heaviest and most durable items in the foundry's repertoire.

#4 forge iron, too, is practically white, but it is very brittle and probably broke easily under the impact of your hammer. It's virtue is its hardness. If you need to score a piece of glass, you've found the right metal. The brittleness of #4 forge made it useless for

casting and it was destined for a forge where it could be remelted, hammered, and manipulated to make wrought iron.

The men who refined pig iron into higher-grade metal used special processes and tools. While they might have worked at a furnace site, most often they were members of a separate industry and worked at forges, foundries, and rolling mills (or metalworks combining the different operations) which were located wherever there was a railhead and the countryside was populous.

♦ THE BLOOMERY ♦

If common pig iron was to be used for work requiring great strength, it had to undergo further refining in a furnace known as a bloomery. The first step on pigs of #1 or #2 iron was to remelt them. The iron was then hammered into oblong bars of higher-grade iron called blooms. A bloom could be resold, or given to another section of a metalworking shop for further shaping.

♦ RANGE ♦

Throughout the United States. Often found at furnace sites, but also very common in industrial regions bordering railheads and navigable rivers.

♦ DISTINGUISHING FEATURES ♦

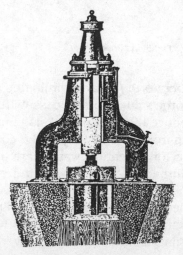

Steam hammer

The early bloomery used a *finery forge* to remelt the pigs. This was basically a huge blacksmith's forge where the iron was placed directly into a coal bed fanned by blasts of bellows- or turbine-forced air. The iron was brought to a semi-molten state and manipulated by the metalworker into rough balls which could be lifted by tongs and hooks onto the anvil of a huge *hammer* powered by a waterwheel or steam engine. Repeated impacts removed excess carbon from the mass and shaped it into blooms. A three-hundred- to five-hundred-pound hammerhead of cast iron was used to forge blooms weighing anywhere from sixty pounds to one hundred pounds. Such a hammer was not lightly moved; if it lost some of its efficiency it could still be resting on the floor of an abandoned and crumbling bloomery.

By the middle of the nineteenth century, when mechanical innovations of all kinds were sweeping the country, an improvement in the bloomery process rendered the finery forge obsolete.

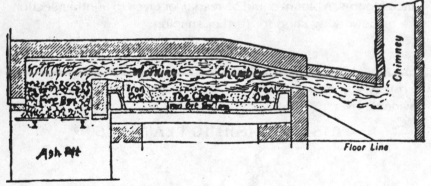

Puddling furnace

The *puddling,* or *reverberatory, furnace* eliminated the inherent inefficiency of the finery forge's purifying process. When the object of the bloomery was to reduce the carbon and slag impurities, the practice of placing the pig-iron bars directly in the contaminating fires of the refinery forge for reheating was clearly not the best solution. The puddling furnace was built with the coal or coke firebox separated from the working hearth by a low wall. The heat of the fire was cleanly reflected off the chamber's ceiling. The procedure of forming the semi-molten iron into balls for the forge hammer was the same as in the finery forge. However, in the puddling furnace the iron never came into direct contact with the carbon produced by the raging firebox; thus there were far fewer impurities in the refined product swung up to the forge.

◆ ROLLING MILLS ◆

Rolling mills converted the high-quality iron of refined blooms into sheet iron, bar iron, and the rails which, from 1850 on, were increasingly used to transport goods.

◆ RANGE ◆

All of the United States, but most common in the industrialized East where rolling mills, along with other metalworking industries, were found next to railroads and waterways.

◆ DISTINGUISHING FEATURES ◆

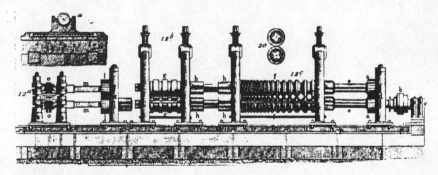

Rollers

Blooms were first reheated in a forge until they were malleable, and then fed through a series of rollers which pressed them into the desired form. Rolling machinery is unmistakable, even if the end product of the roll trains (sets of grooved or plain rolls) seems incomprehensible to you.

17♦

BLACKSMITH SHOP

Today, the image of the village smithy cozily nestled under the spreading chestnut tree at the crossroads is one of America's many legends, and seldom remembered at that. A less mechanized nation honored the smith as a master artificer who embodied rare creative skill and enormous personal strength. His handcrafted ironwares were highly valued possessions in the world of pioneers and isolated farmers. Well-forged tools and implements could make the difference between a successful homestead and an abandoned one, and small objects like wrought-iron hinges were the visible symbols that a homesteader's life was beginning to settle into the rewarding patterns of an established existence.

The coming of the automobile and its lightning capture of the land was the final blow to the smith. He became a shadowy and rather quaint member of an extinct species. Today, all that is left is a cloudy picture of a burly man with a hammer, tongs, and anvil, hard at work shoeing horses. In fact, by the time the car arrived, the blacksmith's profession had already been greatly reduced in importance. A blacksmith restricted to being a farrier—or horse-shoer—was a man being closed in on by a rapidly industrializing nation which no longer paid a premium for his handiwork.

◆ RANGE ◆

In all the states, and in all areas: the countryside, cities, and industrial neighborhoods alike.

◆ **WHERE TO LOOK** ◆

Blacksmiths were a numerous lot, and their skill was called on wherever people lived, traveled, or worked. The village crossroad was frequently the location a blacksmith picked to set up his shop. In a small town, look for the crossing where two important routes intersect; it is your most likely hunting ground. The prized four-corners lots may have been too valuable for the smith's tenancy so cast your eyes on the next half-dozen lots as well.

Major highways and canals of the eighteenth and nineteenth centuries were well studded with blacksmith shops ministering to the needs of travelers in early America. These through roads are easy to spot even though they are bypassed by superhighways and modern reroutings. (See Chapter 11, Roads.) Once again, cross-roads and small towns along the way are your most promising areas, but the regular flow of traffic made it possible for a blacksmith to set up shop outside of town as well.

Blacksmiths were needed wherever there was any industry, to mend and fashion its tools and machine parts. Iron furnaces, mining operations, freighting concerns, shipyards, mills, and many other businesses employed a smith and set up his shop within the boundaries of their operations. Although other industrial endeavors—of all descriptions—may have been too small to justify a company blacksmith, their business was certain to attract an independent operator who would establish a smithy close by.

Large enterprises, such as southern plantations and sprawling western ranches, routinely numbered a blacksmith shop among their outbuildings, placing it conveniently near the horse barn.

The transition from attending to the needs of horses and carriages to repairing automobiles was a natural one for some blacksmiths. The earliest autos were built with familiar features like iron-rimmed wooden wheels, and had simple engines that were amenable to—in fact often required—on-the-spot, jury-rigged repair work. The blacksmith who could create iron articles of almost any shape was the man the first motorists invariably turned to when their cars broke down on rutted country lanes. Naturally, numbers of blacksmiths gradually turned their shops into automobile service stations as their horse-and-buggy trade vanished. There are still country gas stations, largely untouched by modernization, that bear traces of their previous lives as blacksmith shops. Keep your eyes open for the rusted pumps and weedy driveways of abandoned gas stations, as well as the stations still operating at village crossroads.

◆ DISTINGUISHING FEATURES ◆

Blacksmith shops were such a common feature of the American landscape that you might reasonably expect to find many traces of their passing. Your immediate neighborhood certainly supported at least one smithy and the same holds true for any populated area you might find yourself traveling through. Logically, you know you are surrounded by smithy sites, but how many can you name? Don't feel chagrined if your list is a little slow in forming. The anonymity of obsolescence struck the monuments of this historic trade with a vengeance.

The blacksmith's building was an unprepossessing piece of architecture that offered few cogent arguments for its preservation. It was little more than a small, drafty barn or shed that could be opened up to accommodate horses waiting to be shod, piles of pig iron and scrap, and wagonloads of charcoal. It was in the smith's best interest to avoid a building that was too exactingly built; in tightly contained quarters, the constant heat of the forge would have been unbearable. The accessible roadside lot occupied by the smithy was often quickly cleared and built on as soon as the shop closed. Sadly, most of the buildings once housing blacksmiths are long gone.

In spite of the smithys' high mortality rate, their vast numbers means a fair sprinkling of them still stand, generally ignored and anonymous. You've probably looked at several without even realizing it. Here is a remedy that will bring your senses into resonance with the faint echoes of the former smithy's falling hammers.

The blacksmith's forge was the heart of his business and it had to be a substantial brick construction to contain the tremendous heat fanned by the bellows. The *brick chimney* that carried the smoke of the hearth safely away from the work area is one of the clearest clues that the small barn you are in was once a smithy. Most barns and sheds were built to hold bales of highly flammable hay and would never have a fireplace or hearth near their contents.

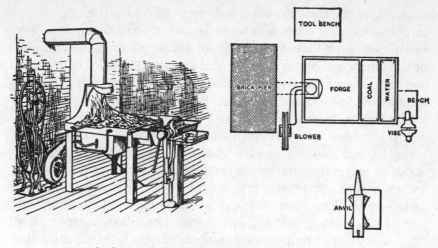

An improved late 1800's blacksmith's set-up. A hand-cranked blower replaces the bellows and an iron forge takes up less space than its brick counterpart.

The *forge* itself was basically a small blast furnace built along the same lines as the large ones found at ironworks and foundries (see Chapter 16, Ironworks). A charcoal fire was kindled in the firebox and fanned by air injected from the nozzle of a large bellows. The blacksmith took the pig and bar iron he had purchased from an ironworks, as well as any scrap he had set aside for re-melting, and placed them in the hearth until they were incandescently hot. He then lifted the glowing iron onto his anvil and hammered it to remove any remaining bits of carbon and to render it malleable and ready to be transformed by his skilled manipulations into carefully shaped objects.

Even if the forge has been dismantled for its brick content, the floor should reveal traces of the charcoal or coal used to stoke it. Some judicious nosing around for the likely location of the storage bin could reward you with a view of the remnants of the blacksmith's last fuel supply.

The New England blacksmith was easily spotted by his contemporaries; his shop was marked with a trademark as distinctive as the barber's pole or tobacconist's wooden Indian. Two imposing granite pillars did picket duty in front of the smithy: One was a post with a small wrought-iron ring used for the hitching of horses; its companion, with a much larger ring, served to restrain oxen brought in to be shod, or simply hauling a wagon in need of repair. As New

England smiths traveled westward, they often took their penchant for stone hitching posts with them, resorting to wooden ones only when there wasn't an appropriate substitute for the native granite of the Northeast. Stone has a way of enduring in spite of weather and renovations, so you've a good chance of finding these early trademarks fairly intact, although they may have been made into gateposts, birdbaths, or other such idle creations.

If your explorations through a sadly decayed barn or an interesting foundation uncover what appears to be a cyclopean tabletop about six feet across and six inches thick with a hole roughly sixteen inches in diameter chiseled in its center, rejoice. You have stumbled across (only figuratively we hope) an important and characteristic part of the working smithy's equipment. This massive stone work table was used to hold wooden wagon wheels in place while the smith rimmed them with iron. The wheel hub rested in the table's center hole and the slab's great size provided enough space to accommodate almost any wheel rolled into the smithy for work. It is unlikely that this crushingly heavy stone has been moved from the shed since the days of the blacksmith's operation. It takes real determination to haul something that heavy and that valueless, so the odds on discovering one are quite good.

Blacksmith shops were the recipients of every worn-out horseshoe and piece of scrap iron that passed within range of their proprietors' viselike grasps. An active smithy was sure to be waist-deep in scrap, with towering piles of horseshoes serving as stock for eventual reforging. If the smithy you have discovered had a decent working life, there is an excellent chance that some of his horde awaits you. A stack of horseshoes or a hand-forged nail puller is hardly a heart-stopping discovery but it is a treasure nonetheless.

Although metal detectors can be handy, they are expensive and are rarely included in the ordinary day pack. A substitute that works remarkably well for many people is the homemade dowsing rod fashioned from a coat hanger. Dowsing rods have been used successfully by the archaeological staff at Williamsburg and were commonly employed by U.S. Marines in Vietnam to locate land mines. By no means infallible, they are, nevertheless, extremely valuable tools.

To use your wire dowsers, hold the long handles loosely and parallel—about two inches apart—as you walk. As you approach a buried metal object the wires will close and form a cross close to

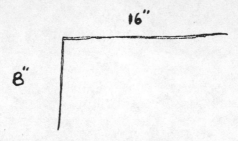

Homemade coathanger dowser

your hands. The shorter wires at the end of your dowsers will be over the find, although, in the case of a small object, the dowsers could be four to five inches off target. Excavate under the piles of ancient straw and fossilized manure that you will probably find. Also be sure to investigate the building's beams and walls for tell-tale signs, such as an abundance of wrought-iron nailheads or a collection of lucky horseshoes tacked around the premises.

The loft above you may harbor an intriguing artifact. Shoeing oxen was a familiar task to most blacksmiths, but these beasts presented special problems. A muscular smith, who prided himself on being able to lift the foot of the most intractable horse, knew better than to attempt the same feat with an ox. It was akin to trying to uproot a fair-sized tree by grasping it around the trunk and lifting. You could raise a good sweat, but little else. The ox sling was the answer: a harnesslike affair that slipped under the animal's belly and was then raised by turning a very large wooden wheel set in a sturdy frame in the overhead loft. Heavy, awkward, and unsuitable for any other purpose, the wheel may still be there for you to examine.

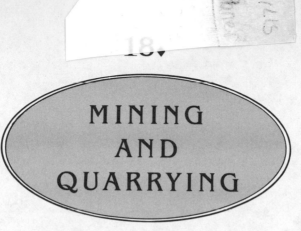

MINING
AND
QUARRYING

The amazing bonanza of minerals on the American continent attracted enormous interest from the days of the first European explorers. The lure of gold and other precious ores would fuel exploration and settlement for centuries to come. Dramatic bursts of mass migration, such as the California Gold Rush, were spawned by the odysseys of solitary prospectors forever pushing into unknown territory in hopes of making their strike.

Humbler minerals actually played an even greater role in the country's development. They were the basic materials of industry and construction that fueled America's spectacular and transforming industrialization. As deposits played out and profit margins vanished, the diggings, which supported numbers of communities, were all too often closed forever, making the ghost town a "picturesque" reality and turning a host of objects into relics of mineworking history.

The great mining regions of the United States are part of the national folklore. There are a score of time-honored marriages of a location and its minerals, and they are easy to spot: Kentucky's coal, Colorado's gold, Pennsylvania's iron, Montana's copper. In many cases the earth is still being worked with the same vigor that it was a century ago and the traces of activity, past and present, are impossible to miss.

◆   **Q U A R R I E S**   ◆

Abandoned quarries can maintain a firm hold on the affections of their communities long after they have been retired from production. The very best swimming and fishing holes are created when their sheer-sided walls fill with water. Indeed, they become secluded summer retreats for succeeding generations of revelers. On the other hand, less favored quarry sites quickly sink into dusty, weed-choked anonymity, marked only by drill marks, rusty barbed-wire fences, and yawning holes.

◆ RANGE ◆

Liberally distributed throughout the country. Small local quarries are ubiquitous; larger commercial enterprises, such as Vermont's granite quarries, are normally well marked.

◆ WHERE TO LOOK ◆

The quarry site may be deep in the countryside, but invariably it will be alongside what was once a major roadway or navigable waterway. The transportation of stone demanded more than the casually tended and occasionally passable country lane afforded. Naturally, you'll look first at street signs and local names for easy clues to the quarry's presence, but should they be absent there are several avenues of investigation that you can follow.

An abundance of dressed stonework in ordinary construction is a sure sign that local stonecutters were active. When stonework shows up in unpretentious houses, cut-stone barn and outbuilding foundations, bridge abutments, retaining walls, and the like, in nine out of ten cases the stone was quarried nearby. The tremendous weight and relatively small value of stone products made it totally impractical to transport them long distances, except for specialized purposes. Millstones, for example, that were cut from a superior deposit of rock might be carried across the country. In scattered instances, contractors for large public buildings and opulent private dwellings might also pay a premium high enough to make the hauling of cut stone profitable.

Cities were the only marketplaces that made large-scale quarrying profitable. The volume of construction in their crowded locations required an abundance of fireproof stone for buildings, sidewalks, and streets. The counties surrounding a metropolis are possible hunting grounds, as are the regions upriver, or farther along the coast where water transport was readily available.

◆ DISTINGUISHING FEATURES ◆

The right angles and regularly ordered step-backs left by the quarryman's work are nearly always unmistakable. Large operations will have left ineradicable traces of their passing in the form of monstrous, barren excavations devoid of topsoil and vegetation. Small local quarries which had a haphazard career may be largely overgrown and far less obvious. Close inspection is certain to uncover the telltale drill and chisel marks of excavation.

The type and size of the rock quarried will give you clues to its eventual utilization. Often there are partially hewn blocks of stone still left, brooding over the plundered deposit. Unfinished millstones point to an important local industry since suitable rock was a rare and valuable commodity. Roughly shaped blocks of granite, suggestively similar to those you've seen forming the walls and foundations of local buildings, indicate that a neighborhood resource was used occasionally.

◆ MINES ◆

There are two sides to the history of American mining. One is the romance of the pursuit of instant wealth which propelled prospectors into the American West. The other is a stark chronicle of the casualties of mining disasters, black lung, erosion, disappointment, and rape of the land. Both are relevant to the modern historical prospector looking for the veins of former activity which lie beneath the present aspect of the land.

Dreams of that one fabulous strike laid unshakeable hold on the bodies and souls of men and women throughout the West. They scattered across the landscape in a fevered wave, leaving faint signs of their passing in many out-of-the-way corners of the continent.

The plebeian minerals of industry and construction, such as lead, iron, and cement, were often not in the landscape of the wandering prospector. The successful exploitation of these minerals could mean tremendous wealth, but it required a substantial investment that was beyond the means of a rude mining camp. Large-scale mining for these basic minerals, as well as for the spectacular deposits of gold and silver, left indelible marks across the land and touched the lives of countless settlers.

◆ RANGE ◆

The entire country. Many sites throughout the western states, particularly in mountainous regions; also dense concentrations in eastern regions where minerals like iron, limestone, lead, and coal were extensively mined.

◆ WHERE TO LOOK ◆

In the major mining regions, it's hard to ignore the constant reminders of man's assault on the land. The boom-and-bust towns, the abandoned workings of solitary, once active mines may require a knowing eye to uncover their secrets.

U.S. Geological Survey maps are your most useful entries into many former mining eras. They show precise mine locations, old roads, trackbeds, and a host of other pertinent information (see Chapter 6 for detailed map interpretation). If you are wandering without a preplanned and researched itinerary, there are other indications to watch for. Major mining sites sired the railroads they needed to haul their ore with speed and consistency. Many, in the late 1800s, were semipermanent narrow-gauge lines which are long gone. Others, however, retain rusting rails that can lead you directly to the site (see also Chapter 8, Railroads). Names with the ring of miners' picks and drills—*Lead*ville, *Coke*burg, and the like—are also easy signposts.

To find the trails of the individual prospectors, it helps to absorb some of the guiding credos which every would-be millionaire carried in his pack along with his grub and shovel. An article of faith was the belief that the mother lode invariably lay beneath an outcrop of mineral, and that the surface traces were but meager reflections of the jackpot below. Prospectors looked everywhere that quartz was abundant for signs of mineralization. Every outcropping, depression, and exposed gully side was examined for rock stained with the rainbow hues of mineral salts as the result of metamorphic activity. That color signaled mineralization and was a possible key to hidden treasure underfoot. Brown-to-yellow designated iron, a likely indicator of gold; black spelled manganese; green or blue denoted copper. Lead revealed itself in a light yellow mineralization and cobalt in a beautiful lilac. Almost any strong color set a prospector's pulse racing, with the exception of lemon or metallic yellow. Lemon was useless uranium, while the metallic shade warned of iron pyrite—the false glitter of fool's gold.

Looking through the prospector's eyes you'll search for those splotches of color, and pay close attention to the heads of washes, or the places where creeks come out of the heights. Every watercourse had to be examined in the hopes of finding the flecks of gold which revealed an undiscovered deposit upstream.

♦ DISTINGUISHING FEATURES ♦

The prospector's passage is rarely well marked. The only signs you might come upon are scattered artifacts like tumbledown cabins, empty bottles, rusting tin cans and the occasional discarded shovel.

Mines leave far more substantial trails. The deeper you dig the richer the vein was a mining principle widely subscribed to. Sinking a deep shaft was a major undertaking and was bound to leave permanent marks (too often, scars is a more accurate word) on the land. Deep mines frequently required stamp mills to crush the ore, railroads to haul it, and towns, complete with stores, saloons, hotels, and all the trappings of civilization, to sustain a sizeable work force. The euphoria attending a substantial strike led to countless mining towns built on a grand scale in the anticipation of fifty years of work. When, as so often happened, the mine produced for only ten years, the ensuing bust was complete; the abandoned and crumbling buildings of a ghost town were all that remained to mark the mine's passing.

Deep shafts form the underground world where men and animals labored to extract a variety of minerals. Many methods were used to support the shafts and galleries of old mines, and there is a substantial body of information on the artifacts, tools, and other traces of the past which are buried in their lightless interiors. None of this will be included here, for the simple reason that mine explorers run the constant risk of becoming buried artifacts themselves. Old mine workings are *never* safe. Rotting timbers, poison gas, cave-ins, covered drops... Enough said. Confine your prowlings to the surface and, even there, watch your step. Mining regions are veritable warrens of tunnels and shaftways. Entrances are often disguised beneath covers of undergrowth or spongy planks—ready traps that can spell disaster. There are ample surface regions that are both safer and just as fascinating.

Most of the minerals taken from the ground in a mining operation have to be broken into small chunks before the ore can be extracted. The lone prospector usually used a pick and sledgehammer to work his claim but a sizeable operation had to rely on a powered mill to crush the stone.

The *arrastra* was the commonplace mill of poor miners working an out-of-the-way claim. Easily built, the arrastra consisted of a circular stone floor of tightly fitted pieces laid atop a thick clay base. A massive wooden post set on a stone pivot turned in the center of the grinding floor and sported one or two crossbeams. Heavy drag stones attached to the crossbeams pulverized the chunks of mineral thrown on the arrastra floor. Power was supplied by whatever was handiest—waterwheel, mule, or a sweating miner. Arrastras were seldom left untouched once their working life ended. If they had been used for gold or silver ore, the stone floor was quickly dismantled by men eager to glean the valuable mineral which had seeped beneath it.

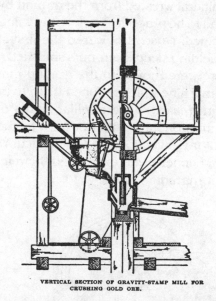

VERTICAL SECTION OF GRAVITY-STAMP MILL FOR
CRUSHING GOLD ORE.

Stamp mills were a deafening counterpoint to large mining operations. Their machinery was simple and effective. A turning cog raised heavy metal rods while gravity yanked them down, a continuous frenzy of stamping that reduced pellets of ore-bearing rock into finely pulverized material. Stamp mills came in all sizes, from the small one- or two-stamp model used in the assay office to massive sixty-stampers, though the twenty- to thirty-stamp mill was most common. The ironwork and machinery for many mills was packed in by mule train. When the mines folded, the worn machinery was often left to inhabit a slowly collapsing building.

Stamp mills were located close to the head of the mine and set into a hill whenever possible so gravity could do most of the work of conveying the top-loaded ore during the milling process. Water was used to power many mills and streamside sites were favorite locations.

The vibration and bone-shaking noise produced by the working stamp mill were terrific. First, metal stamp rods, weighing hundreds of pounds, were raised five inches; they were then moved by cogs which could turn as rapidly as ninety times a minute. Stone foundations and heavy timber cross bracing were required to withstand the stress. The massive skeleton of the structure can tell you it was once a stamp mill even if its works have long since been removed.

The chunks of mineral wrested from the ground by the skill and sinews of miners had to be processed before the valuable ore could be smelted and refined. Muscles powered the first stage of preparation as miners wielding sledgehammers smashed rocks into fist-sized chunks. These were moved to the waiting maw of a water- or steam-powered machine which reduced them to pieces the size of corn kernels. *Jawbreakers* were familiar sights on the mining landscape. Neither unpronounceable nor hard to chew, they were simply the matter-of-fact invention of a Connecticut Yankee named Eli Whitney Blake (a nephew) who developed them in 1858 to provide small stone for macadam roads.

VERTICAL SECTION OF BLAKE JAW BREAKER.

The *assay office* was a center of the mining community, particularly in areas of the West where precious metals were abundant. It rivaled the saloons and bordellos on the prospector's list of essential places. Every promising chunk of mineral was immediately sent to the assayer for evaluation.

Throughout the West, assay offices were constructed following a standard dictated by the utilitarian requirements of the business. A one-story adobe, or frame, structure with a roofed-over front porch sat on the main street where it could easily be found. The building was divided into three rooms. The front room was the office, where samples were received, paperwork filled out, and so on. The middle room housed the assayer's lab. Occupying a prominent position in this room was the doubled-decked assay furnace built of iron-banded firebrick. In a walled-off corner was the balance room which, in order to get a true weight, its caretakers tried to keep dust-free—an almost impossible task. The back room was the workroom, filled with supplies, odds and ends, and the small iron stamp mill used for crushing samples.

Assayers could also be found in blacksmith shops, mills, and other convenient and accessible locations. Their workplaces can be spotted by such signs as racks of crushed ore, or oven pedestals and their accompanying roof vents.

Smelters used blast furnaces, not unlike those in iron furnaces (see Chapter 16, Ironworks for a detailed description), to purify the ore. Their stacks and accompanying retinue of charcoal and coke beehive kilns are the surviving traces of a once substantial mining operation.

Tailing dumps are, regrettably, reliable signs of the miner's activity. After ore had been milled and extracted from the mineral-bearing rock, the residue, a valueless dead-white powder, was piled in ever-growing and useless heaps. Every so often, a chemical reaction of the residue's mineral salts would result in brilliantly colored tailings, but they served no purpose except as garish reminders of ecological spoliation.

The size of the tailing dump is a good way for you to estimate the lifespan of the mine and the community it created. A relatively small mountain surrounded by the remains of immense mills, crumbling boarding houses and storefronts suggests a quickly played-out deposit and untimely financial disaster. A minor Everest of tailings promises that evidences of many years of mining will liberally dot the land.

Hydraulic mining was introduced throughout the West after the 1880s, as the frantic search for gold continued. Water pressure was developed; using wooden flumes and iron pipe, water was jetted through what was essentially a fire hose, to wash out banks of ore along streams. The released debris was then forced over a series of riffles and sluices to separate the heavy gold from the lighter detritus.

The signs of hydraulic mining are all too evident in the western states. Each operation produced an abundance of sluice tailings that swiftly silted up surrounding rivers and ponds.

19◆

POTTERIES

(See also Chapter 38, Pottery)

Among the first businessmen to follow the settlers west were the potters. In even the rawest settlement, a potter was sure to find customers willing to pay or barter for his hand-thrown crocks, pots, jars, and jugs. All he needed to carry with him was his skill, and all he needed to set up shop was a bank of suitable clay and access to firewood.

◆ THE REDWARE POTTER ◆

The clay used by the redware potter was of the most common variety and the coarsest grade available. It was the same clay used by the brickmaker and often taken from the same bank; one person frequently ran both businesses, or they existed alongside one another. (See Chapter 14, Brickyards.) Redware was easy to work, but the resulting pot was fragile, as anyone knows who has ever dropped a flowerpot. Consequently, the production of unglazed, basic redware pottery was purely a local affair. Shipping was out of the question for such a cheap item and little value was placed on its production. The redware pottery establishment was nearly always a small one-man or family operation, catering just to the immediate neighborhood.

◆ RANGE ◆

The entire United States. Spread fairly uniformly across settled territories, with small-scale tradesmen likely to be found in any rural location.

♦ WHERE TO LOOK ♦

Former brickyards are obvious landmarks and can be keys to possible pottery sites. The potter may have worked right at the brickyard, or he may have set up shop farther down the clay bed. Place names are your most general indicators; many a *Potters Lane* or *Potter Hollow* dot the country. Don't bank too heavily on the place name's counsel, alas, as it could well refer to something like "Jacob R. Potter's Lane."

The presence of suitable clay was the main prerequisite for the potter's business, so any hillside excavations that have clearly been exposed to the elements for a long period and are devoid of the vegetation of the surrounding land are excellent clues.

♦ DISTINGUISHING FEATURES ♦

Redware is so fragile that practically no pottery dating back to the mid-nineteenth century is still intact. There weren't a great many redware pottery sites that might have survived and could be spotted today. However, two distinctive traces may remain and still be apparent to the observer.

The *pottery dump* was an ever-present feature of the working potter. The shards of cracked or broken ware were tossed there, as well as a sizeable number of rejects, the result of imperfect firing. Maintaining a consistent heat in the rude, wood-fired kiln of the country potter was a constant battle. Too low a heat produced weak, crumbly wares; too high a heat could warp and damage an entire firing. The "wasters" that invariably accumulated were treated to a one-way journey to the dump. The dump's shards turn up along eroding roadside cuts, in plowed fields, and wherever excavation has disturbed their cover of trash and composted topsoil.

The *kiln* of the redware potter was a crude rectangular structure built out of stone or brick. Most kilns were either dismantled or allowed to collapse of their own accord once they had been abandoned. Some may still be recognizable and languish among the outbuildings of old country houses, or squat disconsolately on the grounds of a barely recognizable homesite that has lost all other traces of its past.

◆ THE STONEWARE FACTORY ◆

Deposits of high-grade clay, which could be used for durable stoneware, were as rare as brick and clay for redware were common. The clay's scarcity was not the only factor that made stoneware valuable. It was as durable as its name implies, and the high temperatures at which it was fired allowed the use of decorative glazing to produce visually pleasing and distinctive products. A jug thrown or molded from stoneware could reasonably be expected to withstand a lifetime of ordinary use, justifying the added expense of its manufacture and its higher price.

Stoneware earth was worth the cost of shipping it to distant pottery works. Usually stoneware items were the specialty of small- to medium-sized factories which produced general product lines to be sold over a rather wide section of territory, in contrast to the strictly local markets of the redware potters.

The stoneware clay was reduced to a workable consistency by being forced through a wooden, iron-bound pug mill which used a series of revolving knives arranged in a descending spiral to cut and knead it efficiently. Next, the clay was mixed with sand and ground feldspar—in proportions varying with the individual maker—and then shaped by skilled artisans working at steam-, water-, or foot-powered potter's wheels, who made each piece an individually crafted article. Late in the nineteenth century the use of molds became universal, permitting the rapid production of standardized lines that could be turned out by semi-skilled workers. For a guide to the dating and identification of different pottery artifacts, see Chapter 38, Pottery.

◆ RANGE ◆

Throughout the country; most early stoneware factories were in the Northeast and Mid-Atlantic states. The Midwest became a major supplier of stoneware, but local factories existed in all parts of the U.S. to meet regional demands for pottery.

◆ WHERE TO LOOK ◆

The stoneware factory depended on being adjacent to an excellent transportation system for many of its crucial operations. First, regular shipments of stoneware earth had to be hauled in. A constant supply of charcoal to fuel the pottery's kilns also had to be received and stored. Furthermore, and of paramount importance to the factory's owners, there had to be ready access to a canal or railroad which allowed the completed products to be shipped to numbers of widely dispersed cities and small towns. Since successful stoneware factories required a fair-sized labor force of both skilled potters and laborers to load and unload, most of them were set up on the outskirts of cities or important commercial towns. The threat of fire posed by the constant inferno of the kilns precluded any pottery location within the built-up portion of the city. If residential and commercial building began to encroach on the factory's site, local ordinances often forced the pottery to move to a less populated location.

♦ DISTINGUISHING FEATURES ♦

The stoneware factory was invariably housed in a substantial brick building pierced by the huge chimneys of its kilns. The brick construction was not so much a result of the potter's affinity for clay as a practical response to the danger of fire.

The outsized brick beehive kiln was the heart of the pottery's operations. A large factory could have several, each one at least 16 feet in diameter. The kiln was built with a top chimney and was ringed with several different fireboxes and work doors.

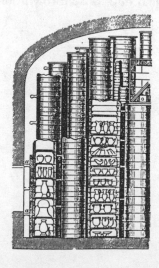

Saggers stacked in kiln

Unfired pottery was always thoroughly dried to remove the moisture that would otherwise make it explode when fired. Fine pieces
were then packed in coarse clay vessels called *saggars*, which were
made so they could be stacked, and placed in the kiln, filling it
entirely.

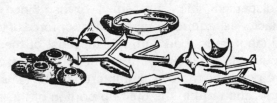

Stilts, cockspurs, watches, and triangles

When several pieces, such as plates, were stacked in the same
saggar, they had to be kept apart so the heat of the firing would
not fuse them into a useless mass. The small pieces of fired clay
used to separate them bore a variety of curious shapes and descriptive names such as *cockspurs*, *stilts*, *watches*, and *triangles*.
Their abundance and the fact that they were throwaways can help
you identify the site of an old pottery, as some might well survive
in the debris.

The *pottery dump* was no less common to the big commercial
factory than to the country redware potter. Even standardized production lines and established factory processes did not protect
against unsalable stoneware which had to be thrown out.

20♦

ICEHOUSES
(COMMERCIAL)

I t's hard to imagine a world without instant access to the ice cubes and cold bottles which make summer heat bearable, much less a world without refrigerators—among the most revered of contemporary household gods. Until the electrification of America, the icebox reigned supreme, and the principal supplier of ice for its well-insulated oak interior was the natural ice industry.

As recently as seventy years ago the commercial harvesting of ice in the United States was an industry, albeit seasonal, with estimated assets of well over $100,000,000. This huge investment was only the tip of the...; there was also a great deal of noncommercial small-scale harvesting done on ponds and minor lakes throughout the north country, which never appeared on any census or industry valuation.

◆ RANGE ◆

Northern states where winters are severe enough for lakes and rivers to accumulate several feet of ice. Also near railheads and navigable rivers in southern and western states.

◆ WHERE TO LOOK ◆

The icehouse site is invariably located next to the body of water that provided the block ice for its heavily insulated storage space. Along rivers, ice was harvested in tranquil bays or coves, or in the deeper and very still water behind a dam where there was little current and consequently freezing was more rapid. Millponds were also likely sources, as were lakes close to large population centers.

As ice was heavy and bulky, an icehouse needed an exceptionally efficient and inexpensive way to transport its wares. Naturally, navigable rivers were the most desirable locations, and the remains of an icehouse dock can be your clue to the icehouse's precise location. On the other hand, large commercial operations that were not on the river were usually served by rail spurs. Look for an abandoned trackbed leading to a lake's shoreline. It could guide you to the site of an icehouse.

◆ DISTINGUISHING FEATURES ◆

The most impressive part of the ice harvesting operation was the enormous icehouse built to hold the cut product. It was a tall windowless structure down by the water, linked to its summer customers by a loading dock fronting a river or rail line.

What distinguishes an icehouse from any other waterside warehouse is the special construction of its walls. Keeping the harvest (and the iceman's profits!) from trickling back into the river as the summer heat wore on was the builder's major concern. Superinsulation was achieved with double-, triple-, and even quadruple-framed walls, solidly packed with an insulating material which was usually sawdust. Unfortunately for today's explorer, when the natural ice industry died in the early decades of this century because of competition from artificial ice factories, the sawdust-stuffed hulks of empty icehouses had a nasty tendency of going up in flames. Officially, vandals were blamed for these conflagrations, but a significant number of icehouse owners made certain their insurance policies were in good order at the time of the lamentable destruction.

The icehouse's waterside location and the extraordinary loads it had to bear when it was solidly stacked with blocks of cut ice demanded substantial underpinnings. Stone foundations, immune to water rot, were deeply laid and their bones are testaments to the past glory of the commercial icehouses.

Unlike nearly all other industrial endeavors, the actual harvesting of natural ice left no traces on the land. First, ice was cleared of snow by horse-drawn or mule-drawn scrapers and marked off in squares. The ice harvester then hitched his team to a sharp, steel plow and followed the checkerboard grid laid out on the ice field. Each pass scored the ice more deeply until the individual blocks were nearly cut free. The final breaking and trimming were done by hand with a variety of heavy, durable tools. Should you stumble upon these specialized implements of the icecutter's trade, you can hazard a fairly safe guess that there was once an icehouse in the area. Such tools often show up, without identification or explanation, in antique stores, backyards, old barns, and a host of other unlikely places. Their presence tells you that a hunt along the shoreline for a likely icehouse site might well be in order.

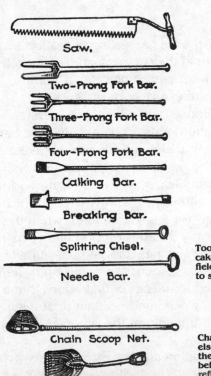

Saw.

Two-Prong Fork Bar.

Three-Prong Fork Bar.

Four-Prong Fork Bar.

Calking Bar.

Breaking Bar.

Splitting Chisel.

Needle Bar.

Tools used to split apart the cakes of ice, both on the ice field and in the icehouse prior to shipment.

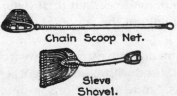

Chain Scoop Net.

Sieve Shovel.

Chain scoops and sieve shovels cleared slush ice from the freshly plowed channels before it had a chance to refreeze in the near-zero environment of the exposed ice field.

Ice tongs were used to hoist and drag the cut blocks of ice in the icehouse, and at every point of distribution up to the moment the ice was lifted into the oak ice chest in the home.

Trimmer Bar

The trimmer bar was used to square the cakes of cut ice before they were stacked in the icehouse and stored until the summer demand.

21 ♦

WATERFRONTS

I n scattered areas of the country, shorelines are slowly being
developed as prime residential property. Old buildings are being
razed or converted, high-rise condominiums are going up, and
contented new residents are enjoying the placid water view from
their windows. This minor renaissance is a recent, and by no means
universal, phenomenon.

To most people, their city or town's waterfront is either a grimy
no-man's-land of factory buildings, heavily shuttered warehouses,
and crumbling docks, or a barely occupied stretch of land subjected
to periodic flooding. The shoreline is a forgotten region, bypassed
by major highways. Once sleepy river towns are now decaying river
towns that wear their rotting, trash-laden piers like leprous neck-
laces.

It is often a challenge to see beyond the current sorry state of
a shoreline to its amazingly rich history. On every hand, the surging
voices of the past clamor for our attention.

◆   WHERE TO LOOK   ◆

Waterfronts would seem to be the easiest of all locations to spot.
All you need do is make your way to the riverbank or shoreline.
When in doubt, a question to a passerby will steer you in the right
direction without further ado. And any road map, of course, will
instantly lay the waterfront before you. All in all, finding your way
shoreward is a simple and straightforward proposition, right?

Not always. Waterfronts have a penchant for changing their locations over the years. Often, in their modern disguises, they have

no more water flowing past them than that carried in underground water mains and sewer pipes. Fill, pavement, and cement can mask a seagoing past. Yesterday's shipping may have tied up far from the current shoreline you have found. Recognizing former waterfronts in their altered states can be a stimulating challenge.

The natural course of flooding and silting up may well have turned a once navigable river channel into a dangerous passage. Riverboat pilots on the Mississippi, Missouri, and other rivers were experts on the everchanging nature of their waterways, and their high wages attest to their hazardous occupation. Because of floods, some flourishing port towns and landings were reduced to seldom visited backwaters, or sleepy inland farming enclaves with barely a memory of their waterfront heritage. Indeed, place-names could be the only clear pointers left for you (see Chapter 5, Names and Namers).

The canal craze of the early nineteenth century created thousands of miles of important shoreline, subsequently abandoned and left to revert to dry land. The ability to recognize the traces of a shoreline and chart its course will serve you in good stead (see Chapter 7, Canals).

The waterfronts of growing cities and towns on seashores or lakes were also frequently in motion. A number of early businesses which occupied prime waterside lots found they had no room for expansion when commerce and the population began to increase. A solution adopted by many was to move onto the unclaimed water itself; by building piers and hauling in tons of fill, they created new shorelines where they could rebuild on a grander scale. This may easily have happened three or four times. The strongest clues are, again, found in street names (see Chapter 5, Names and Namers). What you'll discover, as a result, is not a single shoreline, but a series of shorelines, growth rings, in effect, which mark the progress of a living, evolving waterfront area. Look for these multilayered shoreline neighborhoods in the long established waterfront areas of cities or large towns.

♦ **DISTINGUISHING FEATURES** ♦

Your particular interest is in the shoreline locales that were the sites of early commercial development and activity. In some cases, they are easily discerned because of continued use and a rich melange of historic buildings. Quickly picking out less favored shorefronts is harder; it's a hunt commanding a broad range of interpretative skills.

To understand the unique history of a waterfront area, you will want to investigate it on two levels. Your first goal is a wide-angle view of the land. You can acquire this by consulting a topographic map, if you are fortunate enough to have one handy. If not, it's also possible to get on-site readings.

A broad view needs distance, so head for the nearest bridge that will let you overlook the shore, hike to the end of the nearest point and look back, or cross to the other side of the river or bay and look back at the area you want to unriddle.

The water's principal value was the rapid, inexpensive, and smooth transportation it permitted, and its focal points were those spots furnishing easy access to the land. Ferries, fords, and other crossings should never be overlooked (see Chapter 10, Ferries). *Valleys* opening onto the water are always worth investigating. They'll reveal forgotten shoreline neighborhoods, railroads and canal beds leading to inland markets, and immigration routes that might have had significant impact on the entire area's development. Sheltered *inlets* and *bays* are points where there would have been a concentration of shipping, and towns with definite shoreline orientations would have evolved. *Junctions* of two navigable waterways were certainly considered as sites for development, and should be looked into. Places where streams descend to the waterway were potential *mill sites*, and they, in turn, might well have generated an active waterfront. (See Chapter 13, Mills and Factories.)

Once you've settled on a particular section of waterside real estate, your gaze narrows to the site itself. The age of the buildings you find there will tell you a good deal about the section's development. Home in on the neighborhood's oldest buildings (see Chapter 22, Architecture). If they are in snug berths along the water's edge you have a clear bench mark to gauge the area's progress. If, on the other hand, the oldest buildings are some distance inland, there are several possibilities for you to consider. Fill and reclamation could have created the intervening land, which points to the area's regular and orderly growth. It's also possible that a rampaging flood could have swept right up to the survivors you've discovered and erased all marks of an earlier settlement. If that's the case, the ages of the buildings in the floodplain will be useful clues in tracking down the dates of those former catastrophes.

Small *slipways* where ships were launched can outlast almost all other signs of the past. A common and long-lived way to create a permanent slipway was to sink pilings end on into the mud of the shoreline. Their ranks created a kind of cobblestone ramp made of wood, and its distinctively bumpy surface can still be seen.

Large *slips* produced broad artificial indentations in the shoreline where ships or ferries could moor to unload and receive cargoes. The ability to pull a ship directly up to an onshore mooring was an attraction that waned over the years. Any short, broad streets leading to the water's edge merit a careful look. They might be former slips which were filled in once their real estate value surpassed their worth as shoreline.

Ship-sized rectangular indentations along the shore may mark former *drydocks* used for repair work. Solid cut-stone or concrete construction (commencing after the Civil War) left durable traces which signal the site of a former *shipyard*.

Every major waterfront area, in its heyday, is sure to have had its full complement of *hotels*. Many could still be standing, unmarked and in disrepair. (See Chapter 23, Hotels and Inns.)

Warehouses are standard waterfront denizens. They'll line the streets that are in close proximity to where ships' cargoes were unloaded and then held for sale or forwarding (see Chapter 25, Warehouses).

The local, heavy hauling on land that was so much a part of waterfront life was largely done by draft animals. Any well-used waterfront neighborhood probably still has buildings that housed many of the *stables* needed in a nineteenth-century working district.

From the middle of the nineteenth century on, railroads were the long-distance overland carriers. Their trackage invaded the waterfront area, spreading rapidly through busy ports. The fact that each railroad company maintained its own tracks, terminals, yards, and ferries guarantees there will be substantial evidence of them at all larger locations (see Chapter 8, Railroads).

Heavy industry of all sorts flocked to the waterside because of the cheap transportation it provided. Such enterprises as brickyards, glassworks, iron foundries, and machine shops will be abundantly present. (See Chapters on specific industries.)

Central markets for fish and other commodities dependent on water shipment were an inherent part of the commercial life of major trading centers. Their rambling brick or stone structures may still be used. Or, signs that they once existed might be apparent in bits of wall advertising and the faded colors of storefronts that surround their former sites.

Ship masts and other salvaged pieces of *rigging* from a superannuated era of sail and steam are bound to have been incorporated into the everyday life of today's waterfront community. They'll emerge as gateposts, lights, housing trim, hardware, and in a score of other guises. Watch for them. In the somewhat decrepit scene before you, they are vivid reminders of a time of industriousness and vigor.

Part III

THE BUILDER'S LEGACY

22◆

ARCHITECTURE

America's fame as a nation of builders is justly celebrated. Monuments to the skills of legions of carpenters, masons, architects, and self-sufficient handymen are everywhere, and constitute a major part of the environment we have constructed.

This treasure-house of history is so omnipresent it's barely noticed. Only exceptionally old, or exceptionally ornate, or exceptionally historic buildings rate an identifying plaque. The small percentage of architect-designed buildings are the ones usually described in architectural histories. Most American buildings are casually lumped together under the headings of old (with a small "o"), ordinary, and inconsequential.

To the discerning viewer, these same buildings are extraordinary in their potential eloquence. Homes, business places, and simple utilitarian structures may seem to exist in a senseless jumble of accretion but there is an underlying logic. Each building is part of an unbroken and still evolving time line that links the lives of their former residents with the changing fortunes of their communities and society.

Every building contains more information about the history of the surrounding neighborhood than you can reasonably expect to assimilate. Much of it is buried under layers of siding, paint, and Sheetrock, or simply hidden from your view behind closed doors. The materials and building techniques embodied in each structure can tell you about its past function, the social position of its builders, and possibly even their national origin. Changes in family size, periods of prosperity, and exposure to outside cultural influences are all cataloged in the additions and alterations that are part of most buildings with long lives.

What can you hope to learn from scrutinizing a vintage building? More than anything else, you're trying to place it in context. Your first step is to tack an approximate age onto the structure, fixing it provisionally on your mental time line.

A date is simply a handy starting point for your musings. Once it is roughly established, you can move to the more interesting questions of why a building was erected and who lived or worked there.

Perhaps a casual stroll leads you past a cluster of nondescript, basically identical buildings just down the block. For the first time you look at them with an appraising eye. Their faint Greek Revival flavor makes you place them in the 1840s, but they are hardly arresting from an architectural standpoint. There is little trim or decoration, and varying shades of aluminum siding and cracked asbestos shingles cloak the walls. Why do you pause and consider them with such sudden interest?

The answer is simple from the detective historian's point of view. Buildings do not appear by magic, or spontaneously erupt in a seemingly senseless jumble. There have to be compelling reasons for construction in order to justify the time, energy, and money involved.

In this case, even though later alterations added some diversity, it is clear that the same hands erected all these structures. Sometime in the 1840s there was an immediate need for housing in this particular spot. Nothing you can see from your roadside vantage point readily explains the need, so you investigate a bit more.

The houses were modest and built close to one another on adjoining lots. From their lack of expensive trim or detail, it's easy to see they were never meant as homes for the prosperous and successful. Worker housing, you surmise, further concluding that a fair-sized enterprise must have existed to warrant such permanent construction. You can now begin to canvass the surrounding area for traces of a manufactory or another substantial business that could have given birth to this section.

There are two ways to look at a structure in order to discern its construction history. Nine times out of ten, an appraisal based on the building's appearance will be enough. It's hardly as accurate as a structural analysis but chances are it will answer your questions adequately.

◆ THE STYLES ◆

Architectural styles offer clues that can help you place a building in historical context and quickly estimate its age. There are distinct patterns of construction and ornamentation stamping this country's buildings.

A familiarity with these bench marks is a useful tool, but remember that it is not an infallible or comprehensive one. Buildings erected by architects or carpenters working for moneyed clients eager to adopt the latest mode slip neatly into identifiable stylistic time frames. Substantial town houses, massive mercantile buildings and the like are relatively easy to type and date.

The vast majority of less "notable" construction is apt to borrow bits and pieces from several styles. A transplanted New Englander might be the one who erected a "Greek Revival" farmhouse some twenty years after the style had passed from fashion—simply because it reminded him of his childhood home. Even though there is a definite Victorian overlay, you'd be mistaken to assume that an earlier house was spruced up by later owners.

You'll find again and again that you're looking at buildings erected by self-made designers and architects. Men working by the seat of their pants with confidence in their own skill weren't always rigorously bound to established architectural strictures. The result can be a glorious idiosyncratic display of style upon style.

Of course, structures that stood the test of time were frequently updated when money allowed, or a socially ambitious owner took possession. Windows were replaced to take advantage of larger panes of glass, roofs were raised or lowered, porches added or removed, siding replaced, chimney flues changed for cast-iron stoves—the list is practically endless.

Acknowledging the changeable nature of a building's appearance, you have to develop the ability to look back in time to the structure's earlier faces. After you've examined enough buildings in an area and observed the evolution of styles, you'll feel more confident and your eyeball analysis will be faster. Not perfect, mind you, but accurate enough to laugh at the times you find yourself totally befuddled by layers of later additions.

◆ COLONIAL ARCHITECTURE ◆
(1620–1820)

Suburban streets are often lined with ranks of "colonial" houses displaying machine-made trim and carefully planned standardized layouts. During this century myriad colonial revival houses have been built by people attracted to the early American mode. The carefully groomed exteriors and clearly modern locales of these recent interpretations should not confuse you at all.

In the last ten years an appreciation of the energy efficiency of early architecture has generated far more faithful reproductions. Post-and-beam reincarnations modified with solar glazing and fiber glass insulation are true to both the spirit and the practical detailing of colonial housing. Some of these modern reproductions can be spotted only because they were obviously just constructed.

The harsh realities of life in a sparsely settled expanse of raw land faced all pioneers in the New World. To survive, they had to clear land and harvest crops. There was little time to contemplate stylish building practices and little in the way of local technology capable of adding the niceties of finish and trim to the new structures. Utilitarian buildings were fashioned to meet the demands of the climate, and to be readily expandable to keep pace with growing families.

For the most part, colonial architecture is really vernacular architecture; buildings were erected by craftsmen possessing varied skills and working with limited materials. In poor rural areas, such as the Appalachian Mountains, buildings true to the practical style and placement of colonial houses are still rising from the hillsides.

◆ RANGE ◆

Buildings that are truly seventeenth- and eighteenth-century colonial survivors are found only in the areas of the earliest settlements: parts of the eastern seaboard, in the Mississippi valley, and along the Caminos blazed by the Spanish in the Far West.

◆ WHERE TO LOOK ◆

Long-occupied farmland is the likeliest hunting ground for authentic colonial architecture. Old buildings constructed of solid post-and-beam frameworks or the even more durable stone tend to remain in use in rural regions.

In the country you will want to watch for early buildings along watercourses and old turnpikes and highways.

Small towns and cities are also likely areas, as they frequently grew outward from a settled nucleus without ever experiencing such a burst of growth that the original buildings were razed to make way for larger structures.

Large cities often have less telltale early architecture than you might expect. The constant development and speculation endemic to any thriving urban area can be merciless to structures built when America was smaller in size and slower in pace. In addition, the ubiquitous wooden construction of most colonial architecture was a major liability in any city that became densely crowded. The threat of fire was realized disastrously in Chicago, San Francisco, and scores of other cities. Early buildings were replaced wholesale with brick and stone construction.

◆ DISTINGUISHING FEATURES ◆

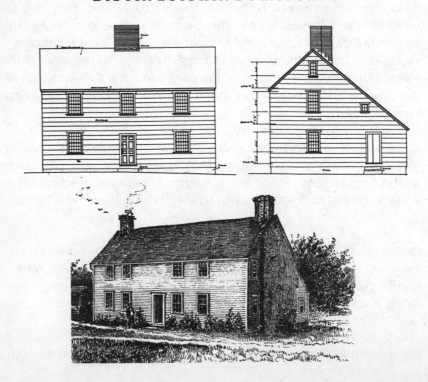

Practicality was the key word for the early colonial dwellings of ordinary farmers and small tradesmen. Often their first homes were little more than small, very basic shelters that offered a place to stay while the important work of clearing and planting the land was accomplished. Later prosperity could mean the addition of a more substantial main wing, reducing the original house to a barely noticed appendage.

In the cold northern colonies, the fact of winter determined the architectural style. The massive central chimney of the late seventeenth-century and early eighteenth-century farmhouse was an English tradition that efficiently heated the rooms flanking it. North/south building alignments were also used to take full advantage of the sun's warming rays.

Southern pioneers, on the other hand, were concerned with cooling, and moved their chimneys to the outside walls of their houses. A central hallway became a standard feature of both colonial and southern architecture, as it allowed air to circulate throughout the house during the summer.

WINDOWS

Windows are probably your best tip-off on the genuineness of an early colonial house. Irregular spacing is a key indicator. Original windows consisted of many small panes, often of very wavy and distorted glass because of the primitive state of the glass industry. Windows with nine-over-nine or twelve-over-twelve configurations are commonplace. Dormer windows are built with shed roofs.

ENTRANCES

Many times, the doors of ruder early constructions are made of wide planks with wrought-iron hardware. They also tend to be small and unobtrusive.

During the eighteenth century paneled doors that were larger and more decorative became quite general, at least away from the raw frontier. Many of them were adorned with a flat transom window made of several fixed panes of glass.

TRIM

Trim is very sparse or altogether absent from colonial architecture.

◆ GEORGIAN (1735–1790) ◆

Eighteenth-century America saw large portions of the eastern seaboard transformed from frontier settlements to established communities. Survival was no longer the residents' dominant concern. Many were prospering and eager to invest their newfound wealth in sizable and stylish dwellings which set them apart from the "provincial" atmosphere of the backwoods.

A formal architectural style, uniform of proportion and material, was the result. Drawn directly from England's style of architecture in the reigns of the three King Georges, the showpiece dwellings of the well-to-do were ornamented and conspicuous declarations that the colonies were coming of age economically and aesthetically.

◆ RANGE ◆

The original thirteen colonies, with few exceptions. Largely in areas of early settlement and prosperity.

◆ WHERE TO LOOK ◆

As Georgian houses were signposts of prosperity, they tend to cluster in waterside cities that were centers of commerce and trade during the eighteenth century. You'll also find the Georgian style embodied in mansions gracing southern riverfront plantations and in the manor houses or large northern estates. Even flourishing millers and small-town merchants were touched by the quest for status, and their less elaborate Georgian homes can be seen in fair numbers across the countryside.

◆ DISTINGUISHING FEATURES ◆

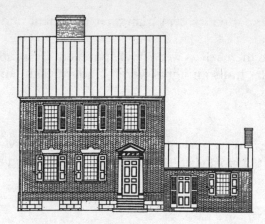

Wealthy colonial landowners demanded symmetry and ornamentation in their new homes. The Georgian style offered both.

Substantial dwellings are basically squarish and compact in plan with a central doorway located directly beneath the middle of five regularly spaced windows.

Early Georgian houses are sheathed in evenly sawed clapboard siding. Toward the end of the period brick was adopted and laid in either Flemish bond or English bond.

The roof lines of the later Georgian houses are not the steeply pitched ones used in early colonial buildings. Gambrel roofs were common, but it is the hipped roof with two substantial chimneys set near the ends that became the textbook definition of the form.

WINDOWS

Regularly spaced; second floor windows are invariably directly above their first floor counterparts. The muntins between the nine-over-nine or twelve-over-twelve windowpanes are quite substantial. Later windows use larger panes of glass, and six-over-six windows became the general rule. Windows are distinguished from the rest of the siding in the Georgian house, and are headed by decorative arches, lintels, or triangular pediments.

ENTRANCES

The focal point of the Georgian-style facade is the entry. Its ornamentation is exuberant, particularly in early examples. Entrances were often set apart by a classical enframement of pillars and pediment, or even set off from the house in a projecting pavilion or portico that sported its own triangular pediment and supporting columns.

The doors themselves were finely paneled. Decorative fanlights or rectangular transom lights were standard Georgian embellishments.

TRIM

There was extensive use of finely crafted wood carving for decoration; and it is most visible in the elaborate molding and detail in entrances and cornices.

♦ FEDERAL (1780–1820) ♦

A new nation demanded a new architecture that was distinctly American and not simply a copy of the mother-country's buildings. The United States was aggressively pursuing its independent course in its economy, foreign policy, and westward expansion. It was through the Federal style that the spate of new construction revealed the vitality and individuality that was uniquely American.

Actually, Federal architecture borrowed directly from the works of Robert Adam and his brothers, England's leading architects between 1760 and 1780. The translation of their themes in such influential American pattern books as Asher Benjamin's *The American Builder's Companion* (1806) effectively masked the connection, however. Even so, there was a truly American wrinkle: the democratic notion that Federal architecture was suitable for all people and all purposes, from the rustic homestead to the palatial urban town house. The adaptation of the style for the brick and frame buildings of the new nation was widespread and added a lasting flavor to the look of the settled landscape.

♦ RANGE ♦

East of the Appalachian Mountains. By the time the land west of the Appalachians was well settled, Federal architecture had been all but eclipsed by the national love affair with the succeeding Greek Revival movement.

◆ WHERE TO LOOK ◆

There is no hard-and-fast rule that says you must look for the Federal style only within its accepted geographic range. Examples of it appear across the country, in small towns, as well as rural and urban locations—a reflection of the general acceptance of this first national style of architecture.

◆ DISTINGUISHING FEATURES ◆

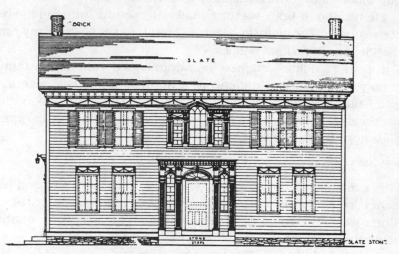

At first glance there seem to be few major differences between many Federal buildings and their earlier Georgian counterparts. Indeed, their elements of proportion, ornament, and layout are closely related. The main difference is in a subtle emphasis on lightness and grace that shows itself in the sum total of the detailing.

The use of semicircular forms that break a building's square mass is characteristic of some Federal structures. Stairwells and bay windows become regular structural additions.

Flemish-bond brick was the material used for most high-style construction. The ever-serviceable clapboard sheathed many rural dwellings with Federal details.

Hipped roof lines retained their dominance without substantial change but chimneys underwent a marked, and easily recognizable, alteration. Federal chimneys are much less bulky than their predecessors. Narrow and rectangular in shape, they were generally set by the two end-walls of the house.

WINDOWS

When suitable glass was easier to obtain, there was a strong tendency to use larger lights in six-over-six windows. Lintels of cut stone with fine-tooled detailing are commonplace. The muntins separating the panes are notably thinner than earlier ones.

ENTRANCES

In characteristic fashion, Federal fanlights crown stately paneled doors. Sidelights are usually in evidence as well. The entire entranceway is often framed by a classical motif of columns and entablature.

TRIM

Carved ornaments and moldings of the Federal period are not as heavy nor as omnipresent as they are in the Georgian style. They are carved in low relief, hugging the surface of the building. Geometric ornaments are the norm, and are generally patera: oval carvings of decorative patterns.

◆ GREEK REVIVAL (1820–1860) ◆

The love affair between the United States and classical Greece was a passionate and long-standing one. A young nation that took pride in its individuality and democratic nature saw itself as the direct spiritual descendant of the ancient Athenians. Hundreds of new settlements were named after the famous locations of antiquity and the settled landscape sprouted legions of buildings celebrating that ideal concept of harmony, the Greek temple.

The style so caught the nation's fancy that it overwhelmed competing architectural trends. Entire streets of Greek Revival houses appeared in towns promoted by speculators, while individual examples of the style filled both the urban and rural landscape. Even humble farmhouses regularly incorporated Greek Revival elements into their structures.

◆ RANGE ◆

The entire country. Most common east of the Mississippi.

◆ WHERE TO LOOK ◆

Examples of Greek Revival buildings are everywhere. The developing transportation and communications networks of the United States swiftly disseminated Greek Revival and succeeding styles across the land.

◆ DISTINGUISHING FEATURES ◆

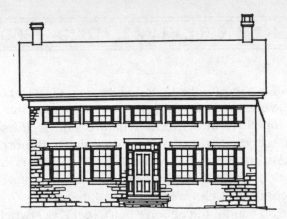

The Greek Revival house in its most sharply defined aspect is impossible to miss. Thousands of them loom like miniature Parthenons, looking rather incongruous in their alien settings. Columns attached to the facade or standing in hollow-wood ranks across a temple front are characteristic of buildings with aspirations to stylishness.

Triangular pedimented gables and low roof line are also typical of the style.

Wooden framing is used for all ordinary construction. Post-and-beam framing is universal for older examples and persists in later rural communities.

Bricks and smoothly finished masonry are the norm for finer buildings, although regional variations influence the materials used.

Dormers are conspicuously absent because the low roof lines rarely left enough ceiling height to make their inclusion practical.

WINDOWS

Main windows have six-over-six lights and are similar to Federal ones in size. Windows are usually well distinguished; they are bordered by heavy wooden molding and substantial masonry lintels.

Typical, and very apparent, details are the small rectangular attic windows used to ventilate and illuminate the upstairs. Known in some regions as lie-on-your-stomach windows, they also led to the misleading and oft used term "eyebrow colonial," which suggests even earlier construction.

ENTRANCES

Paneled doors are customarily used. The stately Federal fanlight is generally replaced by a low rectangular transom light and matching sidelights.

TRIM

Basically a rather simple and stark appearance. Greek inspired wood carving in geometric or leafy motifs can be found bedecking the entranceways and eaves of more elaborate buildings. The heavy moldings that either serve as a frame or indicate a gabled pediment are characteristically Greek Revival.

◆ EARLY VICTORIAN (1840–1860) ◆

The acculturation of America manifested itself in the adoption of a wide variety of architectural forms that were Romantic in nature. Spurning the stark rectangular confines of previous genres, the Victorian builder had easy access to pattern books such as Andrew Jackson Downing's *The Architecture of Country Homes*, published in 1850, which offered an assortment of attractive options. In its early days, Victorian architecture waged a brisk battle with the still popular Greek Revival, and quickly won the distinction of being *the* popular building pattern.

◆ RANGE ◆

The entire country.

◆ DISTINGUISHING FEATURES ◆

Gothic Revival architecture represented a radical departure from the boxlike, largely unadorned Greek Revival form. Buildings often emphasized their vertical orientation with board-and-batten siding, steep roof pitches, and dormers.

A central cross gable over the entranceway is a recurring and typical feature of the style.

WINDOWS

Six-over-six windows remain customary, but nonconforming placement, size, and construction are frequently seen. Pointed arch windows, often in the form of leaded casement windows with panes arranged in diamond patterns, are definitive Gothic embellishments.

ENTRANCES

On the whole, doors are single and fairly unexceptional. Transom and sidelights may or may not be present. Often, entrances are framed by a small porch.

TRIM

Perhaps the most significant clue to a Gothic Revival treatment—visible even on some modest housing—is the trim that embellishes the roof gables. Powered jigsaws and scroll saws had just come into prevalent use in the mid-1800s, and they made an enormous difference in the type of ornamentation available to a carpenter. Decorative bargeboard (also called vergeboard) is a most distinctive feature. Its gingerbread effect is unmistakable.

Cast-iron hardware and fence posts began to be used to accent Gothic themes.

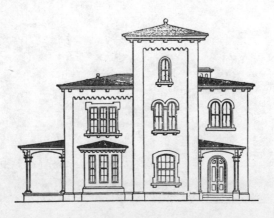

Italian Villa and *Romanesque* architecture was the high-style, early Victorian treatment reserved for impressive buildings. A distinguishing feature is the off-center square or octagonal tower that dominates the structure. Many imposing Greek Revival houses were updated by their prosperous owners by the addition of a strangely incongruous three- or four-story Italianate tower. Roofs are either flat or low-pitched, and have a wide overhang supported by curved brackets.

Bay windows and verandas are frequent.

WINDOWS

In the main, Italian Villa windows are two-over-two, usually round-headed and paired or tripled.

ENTRANCES

Doors are nearly always double-leafed. Richly applied moldings can be highly decorative.

TRIM

Normally, walls have a smooth finish, chiefly of brick or masonry and with little ornamentation. During this period large, paired brackets were frequently placed under eaves as ornamentation. They were widely spaced and often elaborately carved by hand with such naturalistic elements as leaves. An imposing pendant was a typical bracket element. Later brackets tend to be smaller and more geometric in their appearance.

◆ O C T A G O N S (1850–1860) ◆

A truly unique, though short-lived style was the direct result of an 1848 book by Orson Squire Fowler titled, *A Home for All or the Gravel Wall and Octagon Mode of Building*. Fowler extolled the virtues of the octagonal form's spaciousness, heatability, and logical arrangement. A small but significant number of octagons was erected across the country using either a masonry or a frame construction; they all sport a variety of decorative adornments. Their distinctive eight-sided shape makes further identification unnecessary.

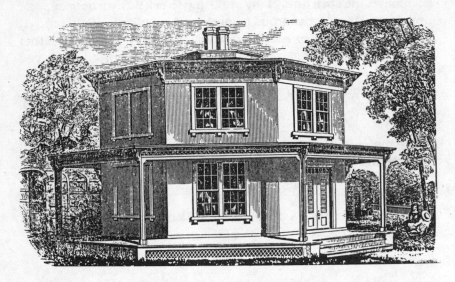

◆ MATURE VICTORIAN (1860–1890) ◆

The explosion of American technology, population, and industry in the post-Civil War period was matched by an exuberant display of architectural fancy and development. The tremendous growth of American cities generated the construction of sprawling residential neighborhoods by speculative contractors. Architect-designed buildings gained an importance they had never before enjoyed; their influence could be seen in the offices of large city firms across the nation as well as in small towns.

Up-to-date builders' manuals brought plans complete with materials and cost estimates to builders throughout the land. With these published specifications as guides, contractors erected great numbers of Victorian-style buildings in both city and rural surroundings.

Slavish adherence to set patterns was hardly a universal practice during a time when innovation and frantic construction were the rule. Although many thousands of buildings were fabricated from precise blueprints, many more incorporated aspects from several different styles.

The complete mechanization of the building supplies industry allowed the construction boom to gather momentum. Power-driven jigsaws, steam presses, and molding machinery were sent across the country on the constantly expanding rail system, as were the products of foundries, glassworks, and brickyards. Entire streets of prefabricated buildings were crated and shipped west to meet the needs of instant boomtowns rising around mining areas or new railroad rights-of-way.

Prosperity and the flood of readily accessible materials provided carpenters specializing in renovation with plenty of work. Face-lifts that practically obscured the original facades of early buildings were performed regularly.

◆ RANGE ◆

The entire country.

◆ DISTINGUISHING FEATURES ◆

Buildings in the *Italianate* style were constructed from 1855 on.

Many of the commercial rows erected in the 1870s are Italianate creations that used the marvelously plastic qualities of cast iron and molded brick to produce heavily detailed ornamentation. Roofs are flat, with emphatically projecting cornices.

Windows are clearly crowned with arches that can be rounded, rectangular, or straight-sided.

Lower stories have higher ceilings than upper stories. Progressively diminishing window size gives the impression of even greater height to a building of perhaps three or four stories.

Domestic Italianate architecture also stresses verticality with high ceilings and towers or cupolas. Roofs are low and hipped with broad eaves. Expensive dwellings boast an abundance of ornamentation.

Second Empire buildings were popular in the 1870s.

This style is very easy to distinguish. Each building is capped by an imposing mansard roof, often made of slate tiles laid in color-contrasting patterns. Cast- and wrought-iron roof cresting further directs your eye skyward.

Actually, the mansard roof of the Second Empire style was also added to many earlier buildings.

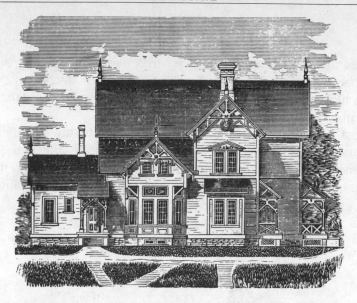

Stick Style reached its heyday in the 1860s and 1870s.

This version of Victorian architecture employs a dramatic array of wooden elements on the exterior of a house to suggest its interior frame. Porch supports, eave supports, and the like also draw attention to the wooden skeleton lying underneath. Roofs are steep and often interrupted by irregular and complicated dormer windows.

The *Queen Anne* style is widely used from 1876 until the 1890s.

This imaginative mode stressed irregularity in its plan, and a compact and lively massing. Towers, elaborately decorated chimneys, hipped or "A" roofs, and bay windows were all popular components.

Most arresting, perhaps, is the variety of textures and color schemes used to relieve wall surfaces of the slightest hint of tedious sameness. Shingles are arranged in contrasting patterns, and many times brick, stone, and clapboard decorate the same building.

Eastlake-style buildings were much favored in the 1870s and 1880s.

Many of these could be called Stick or Queen Anne structures were it not for their distinctive use of machine-made ornamentation. Wood decoration, both carved and turned, is everywhere. Brackets appear in all possible locations. The posts of entryways and porches are intricately machined, as are the railings connecting them. Decorations employing knobs, pleasing arrangements of incised circles, and other such techniques are routine.

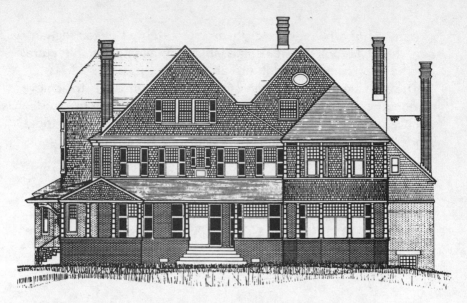

Shingle Style houses emerged in the 1880s and 1890s.

They are readily identified by the unbroken mantle of shingles, from their roofs to their foundations. In structure, these houses were descendants of the Queen Anne style, but they were subtler and more relaxed, spreading themselves on their sites with an almost casual assurance.

Richardsonian Romanesque was a style of the 1880s and 1890s.

Named after the New York City architect Henry Hobson Richardson, this style took the well-established Romanesque architectural tradition and transformed it into an American form.

The exclusive use of massive stone and brick masonry to achieve a monumental effect and the use of low, rounded arches is distinctive. In larger buildings, the encapsulement of several upper stories in arcades to give the impression of a single huge story was common.

◆ CONSTRUCTION DETAILS ◆

Clues drawn from the close scrutiny of construction techniques and materials are sometimes the only ones you can rely on in order to date a building with a degree of accuracy. Exterior cosmetic changes may have been so total that the definitive kernel of original construction is completely hidden.

These clues are particularly important when you try to extract the detailed story of a single site. Information gleaned from construction analysis can increase in value in direct proportion to the condition of the building you're looking at. An occupied and well-maintained house will probably reveal clear signs of its age in its floor plan and ornamentation. However, the fact that the building is occupied can mean that your chance of gaining entry for a leisurely prowl of its innards is problematical at best.

When you find yourself faced with a partially collapsed wreck, or an abandoned and stripped hulk, it's time to resurrect those techniques that help to unriddle a date. Once that's done you can proceed to make sense out of the relationship between the structure and its surroundings and begin to understand the reason for its placement and existence.

◆ FRAMING ◆

Post-and-Beam (1600s–1850 for domestic buildings; to the late 1800s for large utilitarian structures).

Eighteenth- and early nineteenth-century Americans erected post-and-beam skeletons to support their wood-framed buildings, be they humble farmhouses, barns, mills, or mansions. The abundance of wood and the absence of the technology to rapidly process logs into small-dimension lumber made the wood frame the universal construction form.

The methods of assembling massive timbers were the same as those long used in European architecture. There were few instruction manuals, and even fewer carpenters who bothered to track them down. Although every craftsman followed basic structural givens, each man's work expressed the particular idiosyncracies he'd learned from those who taught him his trade. Different means of fastening and shaping were more often a reflection of individual carpentry styles than of different eras.

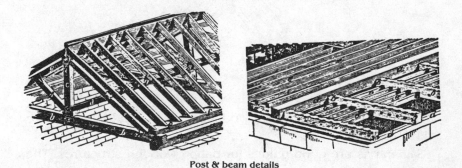

Post & beam details

Dating a post-and-beam frame is a difficult task to perform with any precision but there are some illuminating clues to watch for.

Rafters offer one possibility. During the seventeenth and eighteenth centuries, rafters were commonly pinned together at the top to form the ridgeline.

In the last half of the eighteenth century, ridgebeams were used to connect rafters.

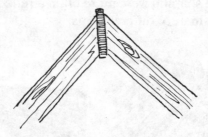

During the nineteenth century ridgeboards were adopted and are still in use today.

Saw marks are good guides for dating wooden structures. The actual posts and beams, which are outsized, are probably un-marked by a saw's teeth unless they are of late-nineteenth-century vintage; major pieces of lumber could be shaped most quickly on-site with a broad axe. Siding and floor planks, however, are a different story. They required a sawmill's attention and along their flanks they bear the marks of the saw's technological evolution.

The earliest boards were laboriously cut by a pit saw wielded by two men. The saw marks will clearly indicate the erratic, idiosyn-cratic nature of each pass. They will be angled and indistinct. Pit saws were used from the 1600s to the mid-eighteenth century in the early colonies.

Waterpowered up-and-down sawmills, often with several blades ganged together, were far more efficient than pit saws, and quickly became indispensable parts of every settlement's economy. The even, plainly marked vertical rows left by the saw's passes are distinctive.

The circular buzz saw, still used in countless rural mills, had been generally adopted by the 1840s. Its efficiency was so much greater than that of the up-and-down mill that it could process huge amounts of lumber and be employed for timber of all dimensions, from immense beams to thin boards. The familiar imprint of the circular saw's blade is unmistakable.

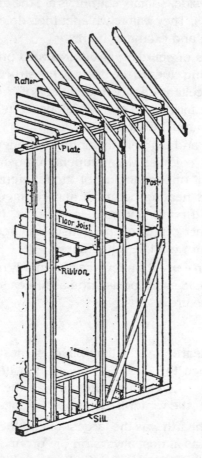

Balloon Frame (1840 on)

The availability of machine-cut nails at reasonable prices and the advent of sawmills capable of turning out prodigious quantities of small-dimension lumber gave rise to a new framing technology. Balloon-frame buildings could be hammered together by a building crew only moderately skilled at carpentry. Easily handled two-by-fours could be cut to size without the highly skilled and tedious joinery required of post-and-beam construction.

◆ CHIMNEYS ◆

Stone or brick chimneys are often the only things left of frame buildings that were consumed by fire. They stand forever, it seems; at worst they collapse into large and identifiable chunks of wreckage unless they have been deliberately demolished and removed.

In the countryside, solitary chimneys are the tombstones of long-vanished houses. They wait to whisper their doleful tales to anyone caring to pause and examine them.

The chimneys of standing structures also provide some of the more enlightening clues to the dates of the structures' construction. There is an excellent chance that many of a chimney's original construction details have been left alone even if the surrounding house has been repeatedly amended.

Seventeenth- and eighteenth-century chimneys built for houses in the northern colonies were stupendous beasts. Their masons had an excellent understanding of the inherent inefficiency of an open fireplace's heating potential and countered it with thermal mass that would retain and radiate the heat. Interior placement, often in the exact center of the house, ensured that little of that precious warmth would be squandered.

The base of an early chimney was commonly made of fieldstones set in clay. It could easily be as large as fifteen square feet—a truly impressive structure.

Cooking hearths

The kitchen hearth was the linchpin of domestic life on the farmstead. It provided the cooking and heating fires upon which all indoor activity centered. The kitchen was the workshop, dining room, and often the winter bedchamber of the family.

The cooking hearth was the largest one in the house; in a multistory house it was almost always on the ground level. It had to be spacious enough to accommodate the crane, pots, roasts and assorted hardware needed for fireplace cookery. The bases of some large chimneys will reveal oversized hearths that seem suitable for the preparation of gargantuan portions of food. While it's true that farm families were notoriously hearty eaters, what you're admiring could well be a relic from a building's former life as an inn that depended on feeding a goodly number of hungry travelers.

Cooking hearths were customary until the 1840s. Their demise came when the American iron industry had progressed to the point where it could manufacture and market substantial numbers of cast-iron stoves. Once this happened, the superior efficiency of the stove sealed the fate of the fireplace.

Sealed is actually a baldly descriptive word. As soon as iron stoves were introduced, scores of fireplaces were closed up to eliminate the heat-stealing drafts of their flues. Some were bricked up, but many were simply given a layer of wainscotting or paneling, in which case they can be found with a little judicious exploration. The fireplace's crane, andirons, and wrought-iron utensils were often left in the hearth when it was sealed.

Bake ovens

Bake ovens were close consorts of cooking hearths, but they led separate lives and had their own history. Frequently they survived the arrival of the cast-iron cook stove and were left exposed long after the cooking hearth was closed and consigned to memory.

A bake oven relied on separate blazes for its heating. A small, hot fire of twigs and sticks was kindled in its center and allowed to burn to ashes. These were then swept out and deposited in an adjoining ashpit, food was placed on the cleaned floor, and the oven's entrance was sealed.

Ovens of the seventeenth and early eighteenth centuries were beehive-shaped constructions fashioned of fieldstone or brick. They opened directly onto the side or back of the fireplace box and relied on its flue to carry away the smoke from their fires.

The inconvenience of reaching across a blazing hearth to the oven mouth, to say nothing of the occasional injury, led to an improved version about the time of the American Revolution. The new bake oven was made as a separate unit and was placed alongside the fireplace mouth. A small flue in front of the oven's door connected with the main chimney. The oven mouth was sealed with doors of green wood which periodically had to be replaced.

From about 1800 to 1850, ovens grew smaller and oblong in shape. Cast-iron doors provided permanent seals and separate ash ovens or ashpits collected and stored wood ashes to be used in making lye. Flues were moved to the top of the oven chamber itself and proved most efficient at drawing up the smoke. However, they also carried away the oven's heat, making these "improved" ovens poorer bakers than the earlier and fully sealed ones.

Smoke Chambers; Preserve Closets

The drying and preserving of meat was an important part of survival in the age before the artificial ice machine. When the time came to butcher a hog, or dress out wild game, there had to be a handy way to immediately preserve the meat.

Small smoke rooms or preserve closets were often incorporated in the chimney base to accommodate a quantity of smoked meat. Today, occupants who stumble across these hideaways in forgotten basement corners are fond of imagining they were built to provide security from Indian attack or were once stops on the Underground Railway. Actually, the very utilitarian nature of these curing rooms would have boded ill for fugitives choosing to hide in them, for surely they would have been one of the first places checked by an intruder, if only in the hope of stealing a fine ham or two.

Many smaller smoke chambers were squirreled away in different places, and were connected by a flue to the main chimney. Where there is a basement, they were often near the stairway leading down. Hallways and landings close to the main chimney body are also likely hunting grounds. Surprisingly, a keen ear can be your best investigative tool, as these cubbyholes, even though papered over, will emit a hollow echo under your rapping knuckles.

If you find what you think might be a smoke chamber of some kind, look along the upper surfaces of the walls for confirmation. Any nails or hooks that were used to hang meat are a dead giveaway. They might even reveal clues as to when the room was in active use if you are able to date the nails.

The exterior dimensions of many chimneys were remodeled in the middle of the nineteenth century when coal stoves were introduced to the household. Coal needed a stronger draft than could be provided by the wide flues of chimneys built to draw smoke from open fireplaces. The wide-throated chimneys rising above the roof lines of older buildings gave way to narrow chimneys which offer no suggestion of the immense masonry structure still contained within the house.

23♦

HOTELS AND INNS

T hey glide by at irregular ten- or fifteen-minute intervals, only dimly registering on your subconscious. Another one appears. Suddenly its sign jolts your memory. There is instant recognition— and chagrin. "Old Stagecoach Inn" reads the display, so faded that your eye is certain to go instead to the neon beer sign in the window. You're passing by a roadside bar with a long history of hospitality, and it's only one of many you should have spotted along the highway.

Hotels and inns marked all the important travel routes of early America. Their large numbers and close proximity reflect the painfully slow progress overland travel once entailed. When you notice them along the road you can look at the community around you with a bit more awareness. You know you're on a route that once served myriad travelers and carried a significant flow of commerce through the area.

◆ RANGE ◆

The entire country.

◆ WHERE TO LOOK ◆

A ride down any former thoroughfare is sure to take you past numbers of hotels and inns that have retreated into quiet domesticity or been put to other uses. The first step is to mark these older routes. A visit to the local library and a quick look at the town and city directories of the late 1800s will give you addresses and descriptions, including an occasional engraving, of many old hostelries (see also Chapter 6, A Matter of Record).

Certain areas are guaranteed hunting grounds. Towns' old *rail depots* always attracted innkeepers catering to weary travelers (see Chapter 8, Railroads). *Fords* and *ferry crossings* were natural locations, since sundown or high water could be counted on to strand unfortunate wayfarers on a regular basis (see Chapter 10, Ferries). *Canal locks* and the small communities they spawned invariably boasted at least one hostelry for the crews and passengers of boats tying up for the night (see Chapter 7, Canals). *Turnpikes* and *post roads* were sure to be main travel routes with regularly spaced rest stops (see Chapter 11, Roads). Even a *town* of moderate size probably had a small hotel on its main street during the days when a ten-mile trip meant an overnight stay.

In general, you'll want to look along the most conspicuous travel routes. Most old hotels picked up a major part of their trade from the passing traffic, and their signs needed to be in clear sight of the highway. Four-corner locations were coveted, but any roadway lot that would be passed en route to a popular destination was suitable. Side streets were acceptable only in towns or cities where there were numbers of transients. In the countryside, a hotel off a main road had scant chance of survival.

◆ DISTINGUISHING FEATURES ◆

Many old hotels have taken on new life as private dwellings, a logical reincarnation as their construction was basically identical to that of other large houses built during the period. Location is an important clue. A house that is just a bit larger than its neighbors and hugs the roadside, whereas they retreat behind front lawns, is immediately suspect.

Many hotels boasted a double porch fronting on the street side.

Particularly wide entrance doors, often paired, are a suggestive construction detail that you can add to your analytical data bank. Inns that flourished before the middle of the nineteenth century can sometimes be distinguished from ordinary dwellings by the appearance of a second doorway leading into a front room from a sidewall.

A hostelry's major source of income came from the food and drink it provided the travel-weary guest, and that required more substantial cooking facilities than most houses possessed. If you find an enormous basement fireplace, smoke room, or bake oven, consider it a valuable key.

Travelers needed facilities to house their teams, so any busy hotel would have had substantial stables close by. They might have been livery stables, long since gone, that were down the street, or they might have been at the rear of the hotel or stood someplace on the property. They could still be there, intact. If not, be on the lookout for telltale foundations or wreckage.

If you find a substantial hotel, it probably means there were several more modest competitors in the vicinity. Hostelries often carved their own niche by catering to the needs of a particular clientele. Drovers' hotels were in the country where they could provide fenced-in pens for flocks. Teamsters' hotels, while conveniently close to the finer hotels, customarily offered cheaper accommodations, inexpensive food and drink, and a much rougher atmosphere. A neighborhood with a substantial ethnic community usually had a hotel catering solely to members of its own nationality or race.

24 ♦

STOREFRONTS

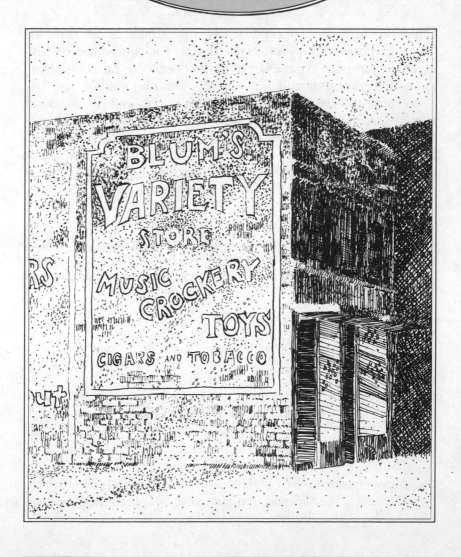

During the nineteenth century, life in the United States centered ever more strongly on Main Street. The landscape of self-sufficient farmsteads gave way to towns filled with shops supplying the countless manufactures of an industrializing nation.

Storefronts were the flagships of their communities. They were barometers of prosperity, and testified to their owners' respectability and "superior" line of products. The story of their construction, flush periods, and hard times is well worth your reading. It relates the fortunes of the surrounding neighborhood and can guide you to other important chapters of local history.

◆ RANGE ◆

Throughout the United States

◆ WHERE TO LOOK ◆

Storefronts are denizens of "Main Street," whatever its moniker. In growing towns they spread into side streets and created a downtown business district.

Early storefronts can appear in what seem to be most unlikely spots: standing in solitary decrepitude on deserted rural roads. There's obviously a reason. Keep an eye out for storefronts in the vicinity of former enterprises like mills, ironworks, or other sizable businesses that would have attracted people. Roadways that were once major traffic arteries also attracted stores; you're most apt to find them at what were once natural focal points: at fords and ferries (see Chapter 10, Ferries and Chapter 12, Fords), along canals and railroads (see Chapter 7, Canals and Chapter 8, Railroads), and at crossroads.

◆ DISTINGUISHING FEATURES ◆

Early storefronts were frequently small buildings of unprepossessing appearance. The shopkeeper or tradesman earning a living in a sparsely populated area rarely had the need for spacious quarters. Inventories were limited and a building as modest as 10' by 12' often sufficed. The one concession to style was the size of the storefronts' windows. Large windows formed of multiple panes of glass were used until the nineteenth-century glass industry began supplying plate glass. Nearly any store prospering into the mid-1800s had its windows replaced with large panes of plate glass which framed and promoted its wares more effectively. Stores with a commercial life ending before the transition to plate glass might be used today as dwellings, their sole identifying feature being the original multi-paned front window. Store windows were flanked by durable shutters that could be closed and padlocked at night to prevent theft. The hasps on the back of shutters, now used only for decoration, can tell of their former commercial life.

The nineteenth-century commercial storefront of the city or large town is unmistakable, and survives today in countless business districts. Granite piers supported many large storefront facades built before 1840.

Cast iron from the vigorously expanding American iron industry succeeded stone in the middle of the nineteenth century. A myriad elaborately molded iron storefronts were mass produced and erected on Main Streets across the country.

Cast Iron Storefront

Architectural details and stylistic influences can help you approximate the date of a storefront's construction (see Chapter 22, Architecture). Fortunately, you can thank the many proud store owners who had the construction date incorporated in the building facade for making a detailed analysis unnecessary in many cases.

The business history of a store is invaluable and entails much more than simply determining the structure's age. Few commercial buildings can boast the unbroken tenancy of a single firm (those which can, invariably trumpet it). The list of different businesses that flourished or failed within the storefront's shell can put you in touch with the past in a very direct way. Local tastes, prosperity, the area's economic base and geographic orientation can all be traced through the roster of past businesses. Your main access to this aspect of the storefront's past is through interviews and documentary research. (See Chapter 6, A Matter of Record, for the tools you'll need for this expedition.)

Wall advertising was a time-honored American business practice that has been largely replaced by the roadside billboard. Luckily, many older buildings still bear the faded lettering of painted advertisements, and they'll detail former business locations, supplies, and services just as effectively for you as they did for passersby of their time. Duck into alleyways separating adjacent buildings and look up. Some of the best examples of wall advertising are now hidden by tall buildings constructed on once empty lots. The fact that the wall lost its public face may well be to your benefit; the old cliche, "out of sight, out of mind," certainly applies to those landlords who see a way to avoid expensive painting and are more than happy to let outdated advertising languish untouched.

Attics and *cellars* of old stores can sometimes harbor long-forgotten remnants of former stocks that haven't been touched since the day their merchandisers went out of business. A few minutes spent in friendly conversation with the present tenant could just give you the entree you need to uncover tangible evidence of a commercial past.

25.

WAREHOUSES

F unctional, solid warehouses are found wherever there was size-able commercial activity. Their presence tells you there was once an intricately connected network of transportation systems, businessmen, industry, agriculture, marketplaces, and purchasers. A warehouse is a powerful magnet for the investigator, laden as it is with the promise of much suggestive historical detail even when its windows reveal only the gutted interior of the derelict building.

The sheer immensity of the simple warehouse in a rural location means it has probably survived. It remains, making you stop and speculate long after the industry or business that erected it has vanished from the scene.

The warehouse in the urban environment is just as much of a signal. The discovery of a single old warehouse, now an apartment dwelling in a residential neighborhood, tells you there are layers of history worth uncovering.

RANGE

Throughout the United States; most significantly along waterways, railheads, and major overland routes. Clustered in cities and towns but also dotting the countryside to serve local agriculture, mineral works, or manufacturers.

WHERE TO LOOK

Warehouses stand in a variety of locales. The begrimed industrial area of a city will certainly incorporate the storage places of many decades of commercial life within its boundaries. They are also found attached to the business places of the merchants and whole-salers whose buildings line the street immediately fronting the water; they will pervade the streets immediately inland too. If the shoreline has been filled and extended over the years, the oldest warehouses could be landlocked and several blocks from the current docks.

Railroad lines collect warehouses up and down their lengths: at every commercial town and at sidings running to industrial works. The junction of several different lines is sure to be a spot where a considerable volume of goods was held in warehouses for trans-shipment.

Warehouses naturally clustered at the terminal points of canals. They were placed alongside basins and slips where canal boats queued up for their cargoes (see Chapter 7, Canals). Major canal towns that were situated at the mouth of a valley or were the center of an overland highway system will also have warehouses along the canal's course.

DISTINGUISHING FEATURES

Early warehouses were commonly constructed with wooden fram-ing. They were easy to erect and served admirably as storage places except for the ever-present danger of fire. A packed wooden ware-house, in stifling proximity to other frame buildings in a city or town, was a very real hazard. A careless hand anywhere up or down the block could ignite a fire. Many a merchant's business vanished with the leaping flames. If he was lucky enough to reestablish himself, the lesson learned was not soon forgotten. In 1828, a transplanted businessman, writing from Augusta, Georgia to a younger brother still living on the family farm in Saratoga Springs, New York, tersely recounted his own too-familiar story: "You have perhaps heard that my commission store and warehouse were consumed by fire about a year ago, and the greater part of the goods which were on consignment belonging to different persons were destroyed. It was the greatest fire ever seen in this place. I barely had time to grab my books and some few personal items. Nonetheless I continue as usual in the commission business, now settled in a stout brick building..."

Isolated warehouses in small towns or rural districts were not as vulnerable to fire, and their frame construction may have withstood the passage of the years. Most of the many warehouses built in industrial and commercial districts after the early 1800s were sensibly made of brick, stone, or cement, just to avoid the catastrophe of fire.

Cast-iron windows and shutters are quick and simple beacons for the warehouse spotter. They secured the stored contents from both fire and theft.

Though many warehouses are starkly utilitarian, a prosperous owner often set his mark on the building, ornamenting it to advertise both his social standing and his business. Sometimes these additions were hard-to-ignore signs emblazoned across the entire side of a building in technicolor glory, but often they were more subtle and easily missed by the casual passerby. Finding these trademark embellishments today lets you pierce the grimy veil of a sagging old warehouse's commercial past and catch a glimpse of it in its heyday.

Starfish ends holding the iron tie rods in place on this 1840s building announced its connection with the produce of the sea, and alert you to the neighborhood's former preeminence as a fish market.

The commodity of a firm specializing in a single product could be subtly incorporated into the warehouse's motif. These tobacco leaves advertised a company in New York City that handled shipments of high-quality tobacco from the southern states to locations hundreds of miles down the coast. Once you have gathered that bit of evidence you can head the few blocks to the shoreline and undoubtedly find traces of the docks, warehouses, hotels, and businesses that were supported by a coastal shipping trade.

The eras' prevailing architectural styles were used in warehouse construction and embellishment as routinely as they were in dwellings, and they can help you figure out the approximate date of a warehouse's construction. For a key to architectural dating turn to Chapter 22. By the time you arrive to investigate a building's paternity, the second-story loading doors might well have been bricked over and covered by a masking layer of paint, but the sturdy hoisting points which supported the block and tackle could still project from the building's eaves or sidewall.

Part IV

A NATION OF FARMERS

26♦

FARMS

Reminders that agriculture was the country's main occupation in time past are impossible to escape once you leave the modern city. We were truly a nation of farmers—from the gentleman farmer to the dirt grubber.

The settled countryside was predominantly a landscape of farms in a variety of conditions. Even where subsequent development has transformed the former pastures and orchards into suburban landscapes, there are often lasting remnants of the original farmstead to catch your observant eye. Farms set down deep taproots in the land and that connection is not easily obliterated.

Land for the taking, soil begging to be turned over and burgeon into crop. This was the American dream of the farmers who settled the land. The push was constantly westward to virgin territory, away from the thin soils of New England and the growing crowds along the first-settled coastline.

Today's farmer is almost an anachronism. He has a deep connection with the land he works and lives on. The chances are good that his family has farmed the same land for generations.

Such was not often the case while the great westward migration was on. Throughout the first half of the 1800s the pioneering farmer was often a man possessed by unslakeable thirst for that new piece of land just a bit farther into the wilderness. A couple of years of heroic toil would claim fields from the untouched countryside and see rude habitations and outbuildings sprout from the land. The first signs of serious settlement and civilization were sometimes enough to send the original residents packing. The farm with its improvements was sold, and its erstwhile owners moved on to another slice of land promising even better prospects.

Often the move was prompted by the inevitable decline in yield that single-crop farming and no fertilization ensured. An energetic farmer could boast of wearing out three or four farms in his lifetime.

Marginal farms with depleted soils were sometimes revived under the stewardship of industrious new owners but many were simply abandoned and swallowed up by the forest. Fields laboriously cleared and cultivated meekly surrendered to the onslaught of natural succession.

More favorably situated farms expanded their central core of buildings and brought ever larger sections of acreage into cultivation or pasturage. The "country" today is a vast sampler of agricultural history, with many of the buildings, implements, and other marks of a long tenure on the land kept intact. There is no museum-style preservation here. There is only the farmer's traditional reluctance to part with anything that might someday, somehow turn out to be useful. The historically interested onlooker can only say amen and thanks to that.

27.

FARMHOUSES

S low down that car! Didn't you see it, nestled snugly in the middle of the block?

We're talking about farmhouses, naturally, those beacons to the past that grab your attention. They exist in large numbers, woven into the complicated patterns of small city and suburban development just as surely as they're stitched into the rural sampler. Once you spot them, you can try to peer through the overlay of later construction and look for traces of the land's earlier ordering into cropland, pasture, and farmyard.

♦ ═══════════════════ **RANGE** ═══════════════════ ♦

The entire country.

♦ ═══════════════════ **WHERE TO LOOK** ═══════════════════ ♦

If you are simply interested in locating farmhouses, obviously the countryside is your prime hunting ground. Farmland equals farmhouses in a very elementary, and generally unenlightening, equation.

Searching out farmhouses in landscapes that have long since shed their fields and barns is another matter entirely. What you must do is look back to the time preceding the region's first energetic development. In most cases, this means you will be looking for survivors that predate the middle of the nineteenth century when the industrial revolution and exploding population began to transform the settled landscape.

Be on the alert for surviving farmhouses in neighborhoods with an eclectic mix of buildings; it demonstrates a slow evolution of settlement and usage. The neighborhood dominated by commercial storefronts or industrial buildings is probably devoid of original farm dwellings, having eradicated them much earlier.

Steer clear of the centers of small cities or towns that were platted with regular grid patterns by speculators (see also Chapter 4, The Marks of Settlement). They were designed as urban areas. Once you move away from that original grid into suburban regions, you are likely to encounter farmhouses that were absorbed into the expanding city.

Older towns and small cities in the eastern half of the country whose histories go back at least to the early 1800s are liable to have early farmhouses spotted in their residential areas. Most of these early settlements descend from a patchwork of thinly populated, pioneering farmsteads. As more people arrived, constructing homes on plots that had greater value as building sites than cropland, the sturdily built farmhouses of the first settlers were often renovated and kept in use long after the rest of the farmstead had vanished.

◆ DISTINGUISHING FEATURES ◆

Your main clue that a house started its career as a farmer's home is its age. Farmhouses don't have distinctive styles or construction details that readily distinguish them from their nonfarm contemporaries. They run the gamut from basic, unadorned shelters to modishly constructed showpieces built for the prosperous landed gentry. Your key is the fact that they were erected before the land was thickly populated.

Farmhouses will look anachronistic in their surroundings. They will be noticeably older than their neighbors and your informed eye should be able to mark them quickly. (See Chapter 22, Architecture, for the information you'll need.) In addition, you can be pretty sure that a surviving farmhouse will be the only example of its era in the immediate vicinity. You'll have to travel beyond the farm's boundaries before you can expect to encounter the next old-timer.

The original farmhouse could well be reduced in status to a rear wing or an insignificant appendage to a later structure, so keep your eyes open. Early examples were rather basic shelters; succeeding generations of owners, living in more prosperous and settled surroundings, could have built new houses that incorporated the original structure.

Farm outbuildings, too, can leave traces that identify a former farmhouse. The barn is probably long gone, but such durable small structures as springhouses (see Chapter 29, Springhouses) or root cellars can still inhabit the fenced-in backyard.

28◆

BARNS

Old barns bear their long lives with varying degrees of grace. Some lie in tangled and forbidding heaps, victims of abandonment and nature's steady assault. Others, as captured by the sympathetic eye of the photographer or artist, stand in quiet dignity. Their weathered siding and air of age soften the stark, utilitarian lines of their construction and lend the landscape a sense of timelessness and serenity.

As soon as you look across the vast reaches of the "country," which still defines most of America's land, you will see that both images are true, yet far from complete. More than anything else, barns reveal their pivotal connection with the work of farming. Their designs, locations, additions, and eventually their fate speak volumes about the lives of those farming the land. A farmer's aspirations, prosperity, and disappointments were often cataloged within the framework of his barn.

◆ RANGE ◆

Throughout the settled portions of the country, with the exception of urban areas where examples are extremely rare. Early barns are often found to coexist with the dates of a region's first settlement.

◆ WHERE TO LOOK ◆

You needn't venture very far into the hinterlands of any state east of the Mississippi to find barns that date from the days of pioneer settlements. Barns are uncommonly easy items to spot. They tower over farmsteads and retain their instantly indentifiable proportions even when they have been converted into dwellings, or are encircled by large-scale industrial or residential developments.

For a close look at a wealth of barns, you'll naturally head for the areas where farming has been a part of the land's history. Working farms, though rapidly diminishing staples of rural American life, are still commonplace, and their barns will doubtless present you with a primer of rural growth and alteration. Abandoned farmsteads, too, are all-too-frequent backroad denizens; their sagging barns are mute evidence of ambitions shattered and harvests unsown.

◆ DISTINGUISHING FEATURES ◆

Barns were built to last. Invariably their walls were constructed of massive and durable materials intended to withstand the demands of many lifetimes of work.

Quite naturally wood was the material most farmers chose, for they spent a major part of their lives doing battle with the ever-present forest.

In many states, the earliest and crudest constructions were small *log barns*. They were easily erected by a pioneering farm family with few resources other than the most simple tools and their own strong arms. A serviceable shelter of alternating, notched logs quickly provided a secure place where crops could be stored, and livestock (and often the farm family too, at first) could be protected from predators and the elements.

Different systems of notching bespoke the skill, patience, and ambitions of the early farmer.

Log barns were staples of the expanding western frontier and never ceased to be popular in regions bypassed by prosperity, such as the southern Appalachians. In most areas, though, their tenure on the farmstead was short-lived.

During the nineteenth century (earlier in the long-settled East), as the population grew and more of the country became well and "respectably" settled, the log barn fell into disfavor. Farmers whose holdings began to show profits after years of hard work wanted more substantial centerpieces for their farms. Local sawmills were able to provide handsome and durable board siding to clothe new barns, while established communities found they had the man-power to erect far grander structures.

The first sight to strike most people when they walk into the maw of a cavernous old barn is the massive posts and beams that support it. Even when a barn has collapsed into a gaggle of debris, the sight of a twelve-by-eighteen-inch beam protruding from the wreckage is arresting. These immense beams are the heritage of the first-growth forests that covered much of the land until the middle of the nineteenth century. Later construction had to make do with far less imposing two-by-six-inch or two-by-eight-inch frameworks.

The framing of the heavy timbers used to support the lengthy spans of old barns is a good example of the individual drive and cooperative spirit that made settlement of the virgin wilderness proceed at a breathtaking pace. Erecting a post-and-beam barn was far beyond the capabilities of one or even two men, but all the preparatory work was the farmer's responsibility. His labor alone was involved in laying a dry-wall, fieldstone foundation—at the same time that he worked the land and tended to the thousand-and-one chores of routine farm life. Cutting, hauling, and shaping the timbers were also tasks undertaken by a farmer working alone, although those with money hired the services of a professional framer to ensure tightly fitting joints.

Once everything was prepared, the call went out to the surrounding farmsteads for help with the barn raising. The completion of each new barn occasioned a joyous community celebration. As neighbors labored together they shared a sense of accomplishment and a knowledge that their entire community would benefit from a new and substantial improvement.

The wooden post-and-beam barn was built in *bents*, outsized sections of mortice and tenoned framing that could be assembled on the ground and then lifted into position by a framing crew wielding pikes and hauling on ropes.

Different cultural heritages have left enduring monuments in their barns. A recognition of their stylistic trademarks can lead you to search for allied traces in the industry and commerce of the region. Although American farmers were eager to experiment with new labor-saving machinery on their acreage, for the most part they left their barns alone and didn't try to alter the form set by the original maker.

There are two main barn shapes, both of which are directly attributable to the influence of European culture; however, local adaptations made regional variations the norm. The English-derived barn was rectangular and windowless. Doors were centered on the long sides of the structure and opened into a passage flanked by stalls.

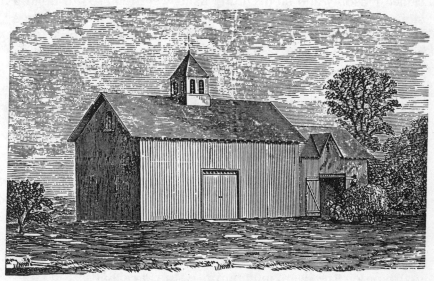

English-influenced barn

German-influenced settlers built bank barns that were set into hillsides, thus creating two ground-level entrances. Also called *sweitzer* or *swisser* barns, they were the dominant style of architecture in Pennsylvania; their example spread across much of the

German-influenced Bank barn

country where the terrain was suitable for such construction.

Stone barns were another German custom, again centering in Pennsylvania and adopted in other parts of the country. Highly skilled masonry and stonecutting skills were required to build a stone barn and they were not nearly as plentiful as the ubiquitous woodworking talents of most American farmers. If you come upon a stone barn the odds are good that you will also find other Germanisms in the area.

Round barns owe their inspiration to a religion, rather than to national origin. The Shakers of western Massachusetts incorporated the circle into many of their creations to symbolize godliness, and in 1826 they erected an enormous round, stone barn in the town of Hancock. It spawned numerous smaller stone and wood structures throughout New England, built by Shakers and non-Shakers alike. Westward bound farmers carried the distinctive concept with them and there are round barns scattered throughout the country, signals of the passage of ideas and people.

The Threshing Floor

Early barns were built to accommodate grain and livestock, often in that order. They were multipurpose structures that served farmers concerned simply with growing enough food and raising enough meat to support their families and with little thought of marketing any surpluses.

The upper level of most barns constructed before the late nineteenth century, was planned around the all-important threshing floor. On it, ripe heads of grains such as wheat, barley, and oats were beaten by flails—a tedious and ancient chore—to separate the grain from the seed head.

All threshing floors had similar basic design elements, developed over centuries of hand farming, that you should be able to spot. When you identify a threshing floor in a large barn, you can be certain the structure's working life had its beginnings in the nineteenth century before the wide-scale introduction of mechanical threshers following the Civil War. Smaller and ruder barns constructed later and still incorporating threshing floors tell you their owners were impoverished farmers unable to afford the services of the mechanized threshers that were a standard part of successful nineteenth-century farm life.

The threshing floor was made of closely laid planks that prevented the separated grain from falling to the level below. It was always situated between two large sets of doors which could be opened on a windy day to let a brisk draft sweep across it. The flailed grain was winnowed by picking it up on a broad paddle and throwing it into this breeze. The lightweight chaff was blown away in a dusty cloud while the heavier grain fell back to the floor, awaiting storage in the adjacent plaster-walled (for vermin-proofing) granary.

Flanking the threshing floor were two mows. One held sheaves of grain ready for threshing; the other received the empty straw and hay that would be used, most sensibly, to bed and feed stock. Stalls for the cattle, horses, and oxen of the farmstead were located on the lower level directly under the haymow and threshing floor.

Silos are such a familiar barn appendage that their antiquity is taken for granted. In fact, the earliest silos date from the mid-1870s and nearly all those still extant are twentieth-century additions to the farmstead.

The earliest silos were either massive solid stone constructions or built of flimsy wooden staves bound with wire hoops. The choice did not necessarily reflect a farmer's means or his industriousness.

Stone silos, while indestructable and aesthetically pleasing, were often built out of necessity. By the late nineteenth century, wood was a scarce and expensive commodity, the forests having been stripped by a century of heedless exploitation. Fieldstone was free and plentiful, and often the only reasonable choice open to a farmer building his first silo.

Ventilation was important to the farmer in order to maintain the health of his livestock and to keep the hay from mouldering. The most common solution was to avoid sheathing the barn's interior in too tight a siding. Cupolas grew popular in the middle of the nineteenth century, and they allowed farmers to give old barns, as well as new ones, an elegant, often Victorian touch that contrasted strongly with the workaday lines of the rest of the building.

Stone barns had to incorporate plans for ventilation into their original design since a well-laid stone wall discouraged drafts and subsequent alterations with equal firmness. The influence of European styles that made their way across the ocean was revealed in the utilitarian slits and fanciful brick cutout ventilators adorning many American stone barns.

29.

SPRINGHOUSES

As you walk through a patch of scrub forest the glimmer of a small stream attracts you. Following its course you stumble upon a curious structure. It appears to be the wreck of a crude stone cabin built into a hill, but there seems to be no reason for anyone to construct such a small, isolated, and gloomy place. Looking further, you discover the cabin's interior is filled with soaking-wet debris; indeed, the creek seems to run right through the old foundation. Everything smells of rot and decay and, given half a chance, you consider abandoning the place yourself.

The plain house on the town's side street seems older than its neighbors and somewhat out of place. In the backyard is a two-story stone outbuilding, obviously used as a storage shed. It's the only stone structure in the neighborhood and looks at least as old as the house itself. You wonder how it came to be built.

In both cases what you have come across is undoubtedly a springhouse, a sure indication that you're standing in what was once the yard of a farmer who owned milking cows. Before the recent invention of electrical refrigeration the springhouse was one of the centers of farm life.

◆ RANGE ◆

Small towns and rural America. Most common in areas east of the Mississippi that were settled before the middle of the nineteenth century.

◆ WHERE TO LOOK ◆

Farmsteads, current and abandoned, are your fields of investigation. Be on the lookout for farmhouses (see Chapter 27) and scan their backyards and close environs.

The spring that gave the springhouse its name and was the reason for its construction might still be flowing; tracing the trickle of a small stream to its source could lead you to the old foundation. Don't dismiss cement and cast-iron culverts and storm sewers simply as modern additions; their existence could be in response to the spring's constant flow.

◆ DISTINGUISHING FEATURES ◆

Built either directly over a spring outlet or hard by it, the springhouse took advantage of the cooling waters flowing from deep under the ground. Even on the hottest summer day, the spring's waters remained around fifty degrees. Farm families kept their milk from spoiling by setting crocks or jars in water-filled channels in the springhouse floor. Some springhouses had waist-high troughs to ease the burden of stooping to lift heavy containers. Springhouses were made with stone or brick walls and floors because the constant dampness quickly rotted wood. The construction was hard and time-consuming but the finished product was durable. The shell of an old springhouse might be the only remaining structure of an old farm. Many springhouses were two-story affairs with an upper floor that included windows, a fireplace, and a separate door. Early settlers often lived in them until they could build more substantial houses. The springhouse was then turned over to the women of the farm, and the second story was used for butter making.

The dampness of the springhouse makes it unlikely that you'll find in it any of the wooden dippers, tables, or other items used in butter making. However, early butter churns were constructed like barrels, so do look for the iron hoops that held the staves together and for broken pieces of crockery that could have resulted from carelessness or a butter-fingered slip (see Chapter 38, Pottery). Other items to be unearthed are rusted buckets or washbasins. A number of churns were operated by treadmills powered by dogs or sheep, so be on the alert for remnants of rollers and gearing.

30♦

ROOT CELLARS

F ood storage was never far from the farmer's mind. Drying, canning, and smoking were vital home activities. The root cellar was another of the farm family's major defenses against winter hunger.

◆ RANGE ◆

Rural areas across the nation.

◆ WHERE TO LOOK ◆

Root cellars were dug within a convenient winter's walk from the farmhouse kitchen, but their exact placement could vary widely. The physical feature you want to watch for as you ramble around a farmstead is a nearby hillside which could have been burrowed into. Some people excavated directly under their farmhouse floors to create a cellar storage place. The basement owes its existence to this most pragmatic practice.

◆ DISTINGUISHING FEATURES ◆

Root cellars are rather humble storehouses. They were built to take advantage of the fact that underground rooms, comfortably insulated by several feet of earth, provided frost-proof, ideal environments for the storage of many vegetables. Root crops like carrots, potatoes, turnips, and such were stored with alternating layers of sand, sawdust, hay, or similar material, against the day of their use.

Often, the crudest form of root cellar was simply a barrel with a sealed top, buried and mounded over with hay to prevent frost.

Any permanent homestead, however, built a more substantial structure. Whenever possible, a hillside was excavated and a small room, supported by wooden or stone interior bracing, was created. The door was never aligned with the cold north wind, and it was made of heavy planks that could be shut tightly.

Sometimes flatland left a farmer no recourse but to tunnel below grade to build an effective shelter. A slanting passageway capable of handling wheelbarrows full of produce led to the frost-proof recess.

You might find a root cellar under a small barn or a shed that looks like just another nondescript outbuilding. If a farmer had to go to the trouble of excavating a cellar in level ground he frequently covered it with a root barn to hold the wheelbarrows, tools, and other items associated with the harvest. Furthermore, a covering structure took care of the otherwise troublesome problems of drainage. The identifying feature will still be that slanting runway leading to the storage room.

While the walls of a root cellar could be simple dirt ones, more often than not they were made of stone and plaster, thus reducing the likelihood of excessive moisture or collapse. Wood was never used as it would rot quickly in direct contact with the damp earth.

31.

SMOKEHOUSES

Gourmet stores in fashionable neighborhoods may be far removed from rural life, but they still herald their "country smoked" hams and bacon. Today, these are treasured delicacies, available only to those willing to pay dearly.

Time was when smoked hams and other meats were the country's staples. Smoking was the most reliable, practical, and palatable way to preserve meat for later consumption. A nation of small farmers depended on the yearly slaughter of a hog or two and the occasional addition of wild game for its adequate supply of protein. It's hardly a surprise, then, that the smokehouse was a habitual farm fixture.

◆ RANGE ◆

Farm country throughout the nation. Also areas of wilderness where hunting has been a chief source of meat for the table.

◆ WHERE TO LOOK ◆

On farms—active or abandoned. Smokehouses were in constant

use until electric chest freezers were generally adopted. The smoke-house will be one of the farmstead's central cluster of buildings and, quite possibly, close to an old butchering shed still displaying its meat hooks. Often it is within eyeshot of the farmhouse itself. Well-smoked hams always attracted hungry thieves or vagrants and the prudent farmer liked to keep a watchful eye on his smokehouse.

◆ DISTINGUISHING FEATURES ◆

Smokehouses were built to meet several major requirements, and their functional construction made them into easily identifiable buildings.

Draft-free smoke chambers were the first prerequisite. To make them farmers used tightly caulked and carefully nailed boards along with mortared stone or brick. The choice depended on the materials available and the farmer's personal inclination. Since wood was normally the cheapest and easiest material to work with, it was the most popular.

In order to smoke meat, a small smoldering fire was kindled and kept burning until nearly all the oxygen was consumed and a thick cloud of smoke filled the smokehouse interior. The type of wood used was important in determining the taste of the smoked product. Hickory chips, fruitwood, and corn cobs were all favored fuels.

A simple dirt floor was the hearth for many a smokehouse fire; however, it was a general practice to dig a fire pit extending several feet below the ground. At times these pits were lined with stones or mortar to create permanent fixtures, but you'll probably find they were filled in once the smokehouse was no longer used to cure meat.

The smoke-blackened interior, the legacy of continual use, is a clue that is hard to miss, especially when parts of it appear on your clothing after you have casually leaned against the wall.

Meat hooks or spikes, set high on the walls or on cross rafters, are dead (pardon the pun) giveaways.

A smokehouse was one of the very few farm outbuildings routinely equipped with a door with a sturdy hasp so it could be locked. Hams and sides of bacon were too portable, valuable, and enticing to leave unsecured.

32♦

ICEHOUSES
(FARM)
(See also Chapter 20, Icehouses
(Commercial)

E lectricity came late to the farmer. It was not until the middle of the present century that it was generally available in rural areas. Before that, the icehouse was one of the standard, and important, outbuildings on the farm. In the northern part of the country, winter saw the farmer and his helpers busy at the pond, cutting out blocks of ice with sharp plows, saws, and chisels for storage in the icehouse. In the South, icehouses were less common, only built if the farm was near a major distribution point for transshipped northern ice or if one of the newfangled artificial ice manufacturing plants of the late nineteenth century was located close by. Summertime excursions to the delightfully cool environs of the farm's icehouse were marred only by the backbreaking task of grabbing a heavy block of ice with a pair of ungainly iron tongs and lugging it across the yard to the kitchen's oak icebox.

◆ RANGE ◆

All states with winters cold enough to cause substantial freezing of lakes and other bodies of water. Also southern and western farms close to railroads and navigable rivers, or cities where artificial ice was manufactured (late 1800s on).

◆ WHERE TO LOOK ◆

The icehouse will be located next to the farm pond if that body of water is adjacent to the farmhouse and barn. If not, it will be one of the closely grouped outbuildings forming the farm compound, probably between the kitchen wing and the barn where the milk cows were kept.

♦ **DISTINGUISHING FEATURES** ♦

The farm's icehouse was built on a solid stone foundation to resist the damp rot that would otherwise have resulted from the ice's slow melting. It was windowless and, except for the construction of its walls, without distinction. Insulation was created by building double walls some six inches apart and packing the cavity between them with sawdust, hay, leaves, or any other handy material. Some thoughtful farmers took advantage of the earth's natural insulation and built their icehouses into the sides of hills, or almost entirely below ground.

Farmers frequently put the cooling microclimate of the icehouse to a variety of uses. On a farm, where everything was patched and repatched, used and reused, and finally set aside for future reference, it was inconceivable that an icehouse would serve merely as a repository for ice. A cool chamber was usually built, or excavated, below the icehouse's main floor for the storage of such perishables as fruits and dairy products. On some farms, the icehouse's cool chamber eliminated the need for a springhouse in which to chill milk.

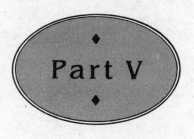

Part V

A HARVEST OF COMMON ARTIFACTS

33♦

AGRICULTURAL IMPLEMENTS

Those forsaken and broken down farm machines, relics from a time when draft animals did the hauling, are now pieces of Americana. They lurk in the scrub around still-productive fields; they lie prostrate about farmyards. An occasional picturesque plow is rescued from oblivion, given a coat of paint, and made to stand as a lawn ornament, but most early farm tools are simply ignored.

Part the undergrowth and forage for these artifacts whenever you can. What you'll find posing as rusted and worn machinery are potentially historical talismans. The history of this country during the nineteenth century is one of massive industrialization arising out of a vigorous agricultural base. The American farmer's enthusiastic acceptance of continually evolving agricultural machinery was a key ingredient in the process.

Farmers' approval of innovation could never have been confidently predicted from a look back at this nation's European forebears. To the restricted peasant class that formed the agricultural society of many European countries, change was anathema.

The American farmer, on the other hand, was a very different breed of man. His ranks included people from all levels of society and there were no apparent limits on his upward mobility. Enterprising farmers were always on the lookout for ways to increase their productivity and claim a bigger piece of America's dream of prosperity. Ingenious farmers were active participants in the industrial revolution as they turned their talents to mechanical invention. A cornucopia of mechanized implements was the bounty that nineteenth century farmers purchased, used, and discarded when even better machines were devised. These are the cast-off monuments you'll find yourself looking at.

◆ PLOWS ◆

The plow was a farmer's most important tool. Unless the earth could be well turned to make it ready for planting, no substantial harvests could be expected.

The first American plows were hand-fashioned from wood and wrought iron by blacksmiths or "plow wrights." They functioned tolerably well in the loose, virgin soil of the newly cleared eastern forest and satisfied farmers working small plots. Every time a plow wore out, replacement pieces had to be custom-made. The procedure was slow and expensive, and hardly began to meet the demand created by the surge of westward expansion following the Revolution.

In 1819, the first cast-iron plow with interchangeable parts was patented; its success generated a competitive and extremely important American agricultural-implements industry.

Eastern plows were moldboard plows made of cast iron which underwent continual improvement. James Oliver's 1853 invention of a highly effective chilled-iron plow set the pace for subsequent development.

The midwestern prairies were especially difficult for the pioneering farmer because of the densely interwoven layers of roots that sodded the rich soil. In 1837, John Deere, a transplanted Vermont blacksmith who settled in Illinois, started the hand manufacture of razor-sharp steel plows from the blades of worn-out crosscut saws. From that modest beginning came a company that is now an American institution. Through the years, and in competition with dozens of other manufacturerers, it has designed and produced countless plows and farm implements.

THE OLIVER CHILLED PLOW.

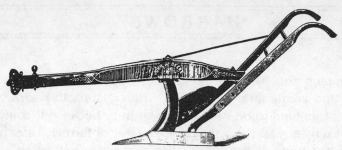

DEERE & CO.'S STEEL FRAME "RED JACKET" PLOW.

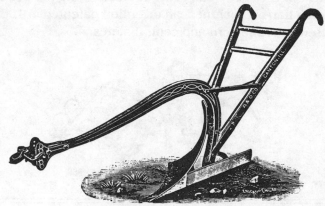

THE CANTON CLIPPER STEEL BEAM PLOW.

After the Civil War, sulky plows and gangplows were popularly used in the West. Two-wheeled plows were general until the 1880s, when most plow manufacturers adopted a three-wheel design.

THE CANTON CLIPPER TRICYCLE PLOW.

◆ HARROWS ◆

These implements, which are omnipresent on the farm, pulverize the soil and create an even surface. The spike-tooth harrow was the first of its kind to be used in this country because it could be assembled by any fairly competent mechanic or farmer. Later ones were factory made. In the 1830s, disc harrows were favored in the eastern half of the country and spread west during the 1880s. The spring-tooth harrow, an American invention patented in 1869, was widely used in the eastern and central states.

GARVER SPRING TOOTH HARROW, 1869.

◆ CORN PLANTERS ◆

Corn planters were crucial to the growth of productivity which enabled many homesteaders in the trans-Mississippi West to establish profitable farms after the Civil War. Because of them, farmers could substantially increase the number of acres they brought into production.

THE HAWORTH CORN PLANTER AND CHECK ROWER.

◆ CORN CULTIVATORS ◆

These necessary complements to the corn planter put large-scale farming at the other end of the spectrum from the labor-intensive cultivation by hoe that is still characteristic of primitive farming throughout the world.

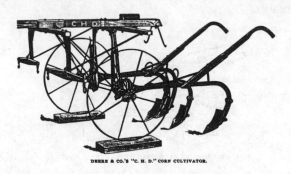

DEERE & CO.'S "C. H. D." CORN CULTIVATOR.

◆ REAPERS ◆

These mechanized contraptions permanently laid to rest the medieval harvest festival during which teams of reapers wielding scythes worked their way across grainfields, cutting them down and tying the bundles by hand. One man operating a horsedrawn reaper would clear broad areas without the help of a sizable work force.

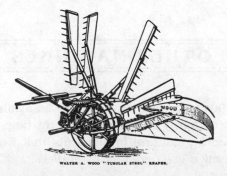

WALTER A. WOOD "TUBULAR STEEL" REAPER.

◆ THRESHERS ◆

Early American barns were built around the all-important threshing floor (see Chapter 28, Barns), but hand threshing couldn't begin to cope with the volume of grain that the mechanized nineteenth-century farm could produce. Threshers, powered by horses or steam engines, that could be taken right to the fields were the modern farmer's answer.

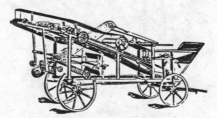

THE SWEEPSTAKES THRESHER, PITTS' SYSTEM.

COX & ROBERTS' VIBRATING THRESHER, 1852.

NICHOLS & SHEPARD'S FIRST VIBRATOR, 1858.

◆ OTHER MACHINES ◆

By the late 1800s improved machinery was available for almost every farm chore. Nearly all successful farms boasted a collection of manufactured agricultural implements that would have been inconceivable only a few generations earlier.

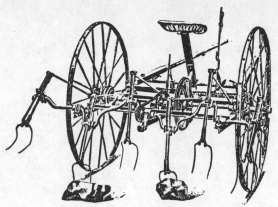

THE OSBORNE ALL STEEL HAY TEDDER.

THE McCORMICK CORN BINDER.

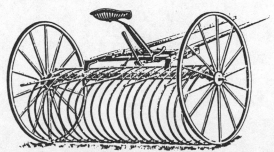

THE WALTER A. WOOD HAY RAKE.

34.

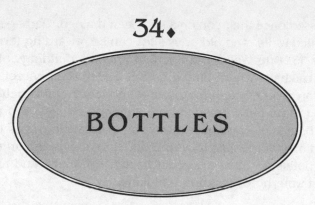

BOTTLES

Bottles are probably the most usual small historical artifacts. They're certainly the most appreciated. Collectors of old bottles are a large and active group whose numbers are constantly growing. They scour yard sales, barns, ghost towns, and abandoned dumps in their search for new acquisitions. Sometimes their forays result in thoughtless plundering and the destruction of historical evidence, but for the most part, they have had a more gratifying side effect. An extensive network of collectors' clubs exists, and for those interested in the history of the glassmaking industry and the uses and peculiarities of its products, there are numerous regional periodicals. The expertise found in them can quickly help you date and identify any intriguing specimens your investigations uncover.

Chances are you will encounter myriad old bottles. They were produced in bulk in the nineteenth century and were one of the few throwaways, no matter where or how people lived. Most bottles held alcoholic potions of one kind or another, from sour mash whiskey to a patent medicine elixir.

◆ RANGE: ◆

The entire country.

◆ WHERE TO LOOK: ◆

Search for places where sharp, glass disposables were apt to have been tossed once their contents had been drained. Garbage dumps, abandoned wells, and old privy sites can be rewarding terrain (see Chapter 35, Dug Wells, Dumps, and Privies). Buildings often had built-in catchalls where empty bottles ended their careers. Check out the areas under and on top of foundations, voids between the studding in partially finished outbuildings, and any and all basements. Bodies of water have always been irresistible targets. Be on the alert near accessible locations like dry canal beds running past former hotels and taverns (see Chapter 7, Canals) and any other exposed waterholes fronting buildings.

◆ DISTINGUISHING FEATURES: ◆

There is a comprehensive body of knowledge available to the researcher eager to identify an individual bottle. Without attempting to cover every base, here is an abbreviated primer to launch you.

The earliest bottles found in America predate the widespread growth of the American glass industry in the 1830s. Most of these were rather simple, free-blown articles. Each bottle was a unique production that took on its distinctive shape as the glassblower's breath filled the bubble of hot glass at the end of the blowpipe.

Everyday green glass was the material almost always used for these first bottles. It was a mixture of sand and either potash, lime

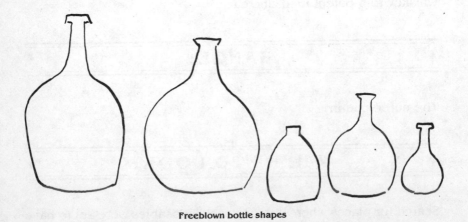

Freeblown bottle shapes

or carbonate of soda. The actual color varied according to the exact proportions favored by the individual glasshouse, and could range from pale blue to amber due to metallic impurities in the mixture. Before 1830, there were few coloring agents deliberately added. Strong blues resulted from the addition of cobalt to the molten batch, greens reflected iron's presence, and amethyst or purple came from manganese.

The necks of bottles are a quick tip-off to the presence of an early production. The neck was formed simply by cutting off the bottle from the blowpipe; it was then polished by briefly exposing it to the fire again. There was no reinforcement to this sheared neck, leaving it flimsy and easily broken. It also didn't cork very satisfactorily because of its slight irregularities. These disadvantages might have left broken and unwanted specimens for you to examine.

Most surviving bottles are the products of the country's vigorous post-1830 glasshouse activity (see Chapter 15, Glasshouses). Colored bottles of all descriptions were made and widely distributed. Details of their production can give you an idea of their age.

After a bottle was blown, there had to be a way to hold it so it could be detached from the blowpipe and its neck and lip formed. Pontils were the tools used to do this. They were slender rods tipped with a small gather of hot glass that could be stuck to the bottle's base. The rough, circular *pontil mark* left when the bottle was broken off is distinctive. Its presence indicates a bottle produced before the 1870s. Quite a bit of glass could be left on the bottle's bottom from the pontil's gather; and hurriedly produced containers sometimes have trouble standing level. For finer bottles, the pontil marks were occasionally filed smooth.

Between 1850 and 1870, several glasshouses used iron pontils that attached to the bottles' bottoms and did not need gathers of glass. These left the bases with circular dimples and telltale fragments of oxidized iron.

After 1870, glasshouses adopted a tool called a snapcase. It closed around the bottle's lower half and held it firmly, hence eliminating the risk of marking the bottom's surface.

Molds were used in American glasshouses to create a broad range of containers with particular shapes and embellishments. Such molds meant distillers and other manufacturers could permanently identify their products and effectively advertise their wares.

Not surprisingly, many a promotional genius made clever use of a glasshouse's capability.

There were many types of molds into which the glassblower inserted his blowpipe, and their ornamentation and detailing varied widely. Some were multipurpose tools with removable plates that could be replaced to quickly and cheaply customize a patent medicine bottle with a huckster's name. Others were one-of-a-kind examples of the moldmaker's art.

Here is a brief sampler of some of the bottle types, produced during the heyday of the hand-blown glass industry, that you are most apt to run across.

STYLES OF FINISH.

PRESCRIPTION LIP. FLAT LIP.

DEEP LIP. WINE OR BRANDY FINISH. DOUBLE RING.

CASTOR OIL FINISH. CHAMPAGNE FINISH.

FRENCH SQUARE. ROUND PRESCRIPTION, or Packers.

FANCY BAR. No. 77. PANEL NECK BRANDY.

Representative bottles from a late 19th century glasshouse. Most bottles were available in varying sizes, often ranging from ½ pint to ½ gallon. Names could be blown in on some bottles for a small surcharge.

UNION.

NEWPORT.

AMERICAN PICKLE.

RING PEPPER.

MASON FRUIT JAR—FLINT GLASS.

GLOBE BITTER.
12 oz.

BITTER.
11 oz.

35.

DUG WELLS, DUMPS, AND PRIVIES

Who in their right minds would throb with anticipation at the prospect of making the intimate acquaintance of a long-abandoned dump or privy? Only someone with a deep appreciation of the historical wealth that can be gleaned from the dirt-encrusted surfaces of worthy, workaday objects.

The discards of a society can tell you much about the day-to-day lives of its people. Dug wells, dumps and privies were convenient catchalls for broken or used containers or household items. Their accumulated debris is both fascinating and eloquent.

◆ RANGE: ◆

All of the states.

◆ WHERE TO LOOK: ◆

All three of these potential repositories can be found around old homesites in rural areas, and in suburban neighborhoods where subsequent development hasn't covered every inch with concrete and asphalt.

Wells were always dug as near the kitchen as possible to provide ready access to the water needed for cooking, cleaning, and the many demands of everyday domestic life. Oftentimes, a prolonged drought, or even the drain of normal usage, caused a well to fail and necessitated digging a more reliable water source elsewhere. The empty and gaping mouth of the dry well was a lure for household garbage. Be sure to check the yards of old homesites for signs of a dug well.

Major early industries like mines, ironworks, and other manufactories often had a substantial dug well, conveniently located, to supply clear drinking water for their employees. This was customary even at many waterside locations where you would not imagine there to be a need. Industrial activity could befoul the water and make it unappetizing at best. When the worksite closed down, the abandoned well was reduced to a trash collector. Look for traces of these excavations close to the center of the workplace, particularly alongside kilns, furnaces, and other heat-generating (and thirst-generating) devices.

Dumps were part of every rural household's equipment. Although convenience figured in their siting, few householders were so lazy that they would willingly bespoil their immediate living area with a dump's graceless and fragrant presence.

Walk a short distance from the old homesite and try to imagine yourself carrying a heavy sack of trash that you want to unload with a minimum of effort and a maximum of concealment. Look for any natural depressions, such as ravines or roadside hollows, where trash could be thrown and covered with a few pieces of brush.

If you see a nearby cliff top or cave, head in that direction. Then, as now, there was something most satisfying in launching objects on long, dramatic flights that ended in resounding smacks on the rocks below.

Towns required communal dumps for their quantities of garbage. Periodically these had to be abandoned lest an overwhelming mountain of refuse rise in noisome, vermin-infested majesty. The entrance to the old town dump will probably be a mile or so down the road. An overgrown track may be the only sign, and the midden itself could be hundreds of feet in the woods, so your chance of stumbling upon it without preparatory work is slim. Some friendly questioning of old-timers and a visit to the local archives are definitely in order (see Chapter 6, A Matter of Record).

Privies were always but a short stroll from the back door. The exact distance between the house and outhouse was a delicate decision, made only after considering the prevailing winds, the winters' severity, and the intestinal fortitude of the prospective users.

Outhouses were ready litter baskets for empty bottles, broken crockery, and any other small item that could be dropped into them. Privies had to be moved regularly and new pits dug as their odorous contents crept toward the rude wooden seat which was the privy's throne. As a result, there may be several long-forgotten sites within a short distance of each other.

◆ DISTINGUISHING FEATURES: ◆

Most of these old collectors of trash have been filled in and reveal themselves only by telltale differences from the surrounding soil (see Chapter 2, The Soil's Story). Wells are the receptacles most apt to retain clear markings as they were encircled by a low, carefully mortared wall of stone or brick that might still be standing. Most of the other distinguishing features of wells, dumps, and privies are, in fact, siting factors, and those we have already covered. That being the case, it seems appropriate to use this space to discuss the controversy over the treasure hunter.

You'll discover competition—at times intense—when you rummage through old dumping grounds. Yesterday's discards are today's collectibles and often bear a high market value. Bottle collectors are the most pervasive hunters. Armed with shovels and voracious appetites for finds, they are sure to appear at any site you might uncover.

Such foraging horrifies many professional historians and archaeologists. As you must certainly know, random objects removed from their historical context don't contribute very much to an understanding of the time and place from which they came. Still, they do reveal more above ground than they would lying buried and undiscovered.

The sheer number of potential dumps guarantees that only a

few of them will ever be examined by professionals with the skill to thoroughly record their excavations. By taking notes on the depth at which you unearth various items, and by chronicling your progress with a series of photos, you can proceed with a clear conscience when you're looking through a run-of-the-mill, nineteenth-century dumping ground. Your observations and interest in the historical context of your finds can only add to public knowledge.

However, there are finds that you should scrupulously avoid in order not to do serious historical damage. Any significant finds predating the nineteenth century should be left alone and brought to the attention of your state historical society. They'll help you determine whether the site you are examining is ever apt to be targeted for serious excavation. In areas of the country where settlement occurred during the nineteenth century, you should refrain from disturbing any sites that might be those of early arrivals.

Native American sites are the proper domain of trained archaeologists. Let them know when your intelligent reconnaissance uncovers one and you will be well repaid by their gratitude.

Your own sense of a location's historical importance is your best guide. Follow your informed evaluation with an intelligent degree of caution and steer clear of any excavation that might obscure an important chapter in local history. Surely that's the last thing you'd want to do, and there are scores of safe locations for you to explore and learn from.

36♦

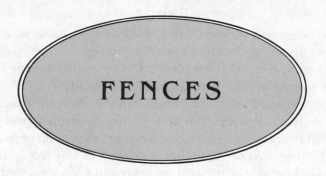

FENCES

"Good fences make good neighbors" goes the old saw, but for the farmer trying to establish himself on the raw land, neighbors hardly entered the picture. Fences were built to keep the livestock out of those fields which had been claimed for cultivation after long days of backbreaking effort. At the same time, they were built to keep the precious livestock from straying into the woods where it could fall prey to wild animals or hungry men. Life was risky enough without courting starvation by not putting up a reasonable fence around your fields. Once you were well-established and felt a bit less precarious you could reflect on the property claim your fences upheld, and only then begin to worry about neighbors who might covet your land and its production.

Fortunately, fencing material was available in abundance to the pioneering American farmers who opened up the eastern half of the country to settlement. Life was a constant battle with the endless forest, so wood was plentiful. Fences made of pulled stumps or posts and rails were used in a variety of combinations. Unfortunately, those original barriers have left few traces for today's observer to discover. Wooden fences had limited life-spans and had to be constantly replaced as insects and decay did their best to return them to the humus of the soil. About all you can do to find the lie of old wooden fences is to look for marker trees (see Chapter 3, Plant Language) and imagine the former rows of fences stretching between them. Other kinds of fencing, however, left more lasting impressions on the land, and are waiting to tell you about the former shape of the land they enclose.

◆ STONE WALLS ◆

◆ Range ◆

The Northeast and Middle Atlantic states where rocky soil yielded abundant material. Scattered widely throughout the rest of the country; often erected in the West by transplanted Yankee farmers as testimonials to their New England farmsteads.

In the Northeast, stone walls became the standard fencing material almost by default. The soil of New England farms was so rocky that every plowing unearthed a small mountain of stone that had to be disposed of. As the plow worked its way along the field, the farmer pitched the mineral harvest onto a wooden sled known as a stoneboat, which was then hitched to a team and the material hauled to the edge of the field to be dumped. Depending on the temperament of the farmer, this pile of stones could assume different forms. It could slowly be transformed into a carefully laid and enduring monument to the farmer's skill and enterprise, or it could be hurriedly tossed into an equally permanent but ruder wall. Sometimes the stone harvest was so prolific that a towering cairn of stones appeared in a handy and relatively worthless corner, a bewilderment to the latter-day hiker who stumbles across it and imagines an ancient temple in a forgotten civilization.

Today, stone walls are often found stretching interminably through what seems to be untouched forest. When you see a stone wall, you can be sure that the land under your feet was once cleared farmland and that the present woodland is probably the product of decades of neglect.

A perplexing stone wall that weaves through the forest in a zigzag line immortalizes the path of an earlier wooden-snake fence. As stones were cleared from the field they were piled against the surrounding fence line and eventually formed a permanent barrier. When the wood had rotted away, the piled stones remained.

◆ LIVING FENCES ◆

◆ Range ◆

Prairie and western states; portions of the South from Georgia to Texas.

LEAVES AND FRUIT OF OSAGE ORANGE.

The westward push of pioneering farmers came to an abrupt halt when they encountered the vast treeless expanse of the prairie. Men inured to constant battle with the forest had to adjust to a world where wood was a precious commodity and even stones were sparse. Finding a suitable fence to protect the crops and livestock was a pressing and much discussed problem. Some farmers laboriously stacked cut sod into fences or piled brush into flimsy barricades, but the overwhelming response was dismay, until the late 1860s and early 1870s when a marvelous answer seemed to be found. Hedges were heralded as the perfect solution for the fertile yet treeless prairie. A variety of plants was tested as eager farmers experimented in their search for the ideal fence. Cherokee rose gained a certain favor in the South and was planted extensively. Honey locust, thorny locust, and numerous varieties of promising local plants were also tried, but all were set aside when the almost perfect plant was found. The undisputed king of the hedgerows was the Osage Orange. Its wood was immensely strong, flexible and almost impervious to rot. These attributes made it the American Indians' favorite wood for bows and war clubs, and gave rise to its less familiar names: "bois d'arc" (reflecting French exploration of the Louisiana territory) and "bowwood." More importantly, the plant grew quickly, shrugging off heat, cold, and drought with ease. Then, too, it was clothed in armor of lethal spines. In short, it guaranteed the consummate fence—"horse high, bull strong, and pig tight." The only major drawbacks to the Osage Orange fence were the four or five years it took to grow large enough to deter stock; the fact that an established fence couldn't be moved; and its vulnerability to prairie fires. With the introduction of barbed wire in the 1880s, the Osage Orange quickly became an anachronism with no place on most farmers' and ranchers' property.

◆ WHERE TO LOOK ◆

Originally Osage Orange was native only to a small region of the country near Arkansas and southern Missouri. However, the demand for seeds created a large local industry there and as a result, hedgerows were planted in the prairie states from Illinois to Texas. Scattered stands are still found throughout the country.

You are apt to find survivors near houses where a section of hedge was kept for its ornamental and windbreak value or along the far edges of fields where it was more trouble to eradicate than to live with. The hard, orange-yellow wood of the Osage Orange made the best of all fence posts. Practically rotproof, Osage Orange fence posts can still be seen marking the location of a former hedgerow, but their own thorny branches have been replaced with strands of barbed wire.

◆ IRON (WROUGHT AND CAST) ◆

◆ RANGE ◆

The entire country; both urban and rural.

From a very early date the houses of the well-to-do and the grounds of important public buildings like the church and town hall were guarded by iron fencing. The metal barrier was a declaration of prosperity and permanence that had little in common with the utilitarian fencing of the pioneer farmer.

Iron fences were monuments to the cultivation and refinement of the men who commissioned them, visible proof of their successful ascension of the social ladder. Far more expensive to erect than any other construction, iron fencing was suitable for small city and town lots, community cemeteries and parks, and the short roadside frontage of the prosperous farmhouse.

◆ WHERE TO LOOK ◆

Iron fences cluster in small towns and cities where lots of modest dimensions could be enclosed by durable and decorative fences. Areas with residential and commercial centers that prospered in the nineteenth century are abundantly fertile grounds. If you do run across an enduring iron fence guarding the yard of a rundown and seemingly undistinguished old tenement, remember that its past could be quite grand.

Churches and cemeteries active during the nineteenth century often hold specimens of iron fencing in their precincts, giving them sanctuary from the depredations of scavengers and vandals. Rural congregations are as likely to be blessed with fine examples as urban ones. The family plots of prominent citizens are often marked by an iron perimeter.

◆ DISTINGUISHING FEATURES ◆

Wrought-Iron Fences

The earliest metal fences were nearly always fashioned of wrought iron. Bars of malleable iron were hammered, twisted, and shaped at the blacksmith's forge into practically indestructable fence sections. Most of this fencing still bears the imprint of the hammer-blows that shaped it and clearly reveals its handwrought nature in its lack of perfect symmetry. Each piece is a unique, and often remarkably pleasing, construction.

Wrought-iron fences were (and still are) the most expensive kind of fence to erect because of the labor involved in their creation. Each component in their design had to be individually shaped and joined by the blacksmith and his assistants. As a result, most wrought-iron fences were built to rather simple patterns.

Elaborate and often strikingly beautiful work was normally reserved for the gate fronting an elegant town house or a major public building.

Dating a wrought-iron fence is an arduous task at best. Only a specially commissioned piece came complete with information about its creator and its date. Most work was unsigned, undated, and generally bereft of identifying features.

Your best bet is to study the location of the fence and try to date the structure, or the area it surrounds. Even this is far from foolproof because of the enduring quality of wrought iron. Hand-tooled fences have a disconcerting way of outlasting the buildings they originally encircled. They are frequently removed and subsequently erected around later construction.

◆ CAST-IRON FENCES ◆

The development of the American iron industry in the first half of the nineteenth century (see Chapter 16, Ironworks) made prestigious iron fencing accessible to an ever-growing number of successful merchants, farmers, and professionals. Across the nation, foundries fired up their furnaces and poured molten iron into fence molds carefully placed on the casting floor.

Cast-iron fences were still relatively expensive items, but they were all within the reach of the moderately affluent consumer who wanted to add a touch of class to his house or property.

The least costly iron fence to manufacture was poured into an open mold at the foundry. The side of the fencing presenting an imposing exterior to the passerby revealed the finished detail of the pattern. The side turned to the owner was bland and featureless.

Cast-iron fences can be dated quite readily by the style of their construction. Early cast iron from the first decades of the nineteenth century was based on simple wrought-iron designs and thought of as an inexpensive substitute for existing materials.

Founders, realizing there was no reason to limit themselves to simple designs, soon began embellishing their product. The result was an amazing diversity of design that far surpassed what could be fashioned from the wrought-iron technique.

Each foundry had its own catalog and there was constant copying and adaptation of existing designs. Pattern books like Asher Benjamin's 1833 *Practice of Architecture* furnished models for the foundries of the major eastern cities producing ornamental ironwork. As settlement broadened westward in the 1840s and 1850s, the pattern books were packed in pioneers' cargoes and their influence spread to interior settlements.

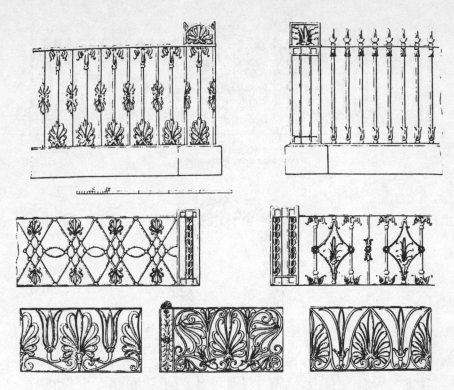

Patterns from Asher Benjamin's widely read *Practice of Architecture* (1833)

The work of individual foundries is almost impossible to determine in the absence of a nameplate, but you can reach an educated guess of the date of manufacture by examining the casting styles.

During the 1830s and 1840s the rapidly expanding iron industry was heavily influenced by the nation's enthusiasm for the classical revival movement. Greek revival houses were gracing the countryside in scores and their ornamental iron fences reinforced the classical theme.

The founders' imaginative floodgates burst open during the Victorian era, from the 1850s to the close of the century. A plethora of decoration was added to the iron fence, completing the transformation from the restrained example set by the blacksmith's handiwork. Gothic arches, gargoyles, and plants (often local favorites like corn and sunflowers) adorned dwellings, public buildings, and cemeteries in mind-boggling profusion.

No. 201.
WOOD & PEROT, Philadelphia,

1858 Victorian enthusiasm

♦ **BARBED WIRE** ♦

Barbed-wire fencing is a post-Civil War invention. The first patent was granted in 1868 but commercial production did not commence until 1874 when ten miles of wire were manufactured. Ten years later, in 1884, barbed wire had established itself as the preferred fencing of the American farmer and rancher. More than 250,000 miles of it were manufactured that year alone, reflecting a sustained and vigorous demand.

The new fencing had a lot to recommend it. It was much cheaper to build a wire fence than any other kind, both in material and in labor. Installation was simple and the fence lasted well. A farm surrounded by thousands of feet of wooden fence demanded constant vigilance as posts and cross members rotted and had to be replaced with wood, laboriously cut and split for the purpose. Barbed wire provided a reliable fence needing only routine inspection and perhaps an easy, on-the-spot repair or two.

At first, farmers were daunted by the treeless western prairies where they were unable to find fencing. Not so the cattlemen who drove immense herds of cattle across the open range to distant markets. Barbed wire ended that era and ushered in a more orderly, settled way of life, but the transition was bloody and abrupt. Cattlemen scorned farmers' initial attempts to enclose their lands and protect their crops from the passing cattle drives. "Nesters," they contemptuously called them as they summarily went about fence cutting. With startling rapidity the cattle routes were blocked by not one, but hundreds of fenced property lines. Contempt changed to desperation and barbed wire became the cause célèbre of the cattle-sheep wars that made Billy the Kid and other gunfighters notorious. The cattle interests fought, but wire, farming, and settlement won.

At the same time, an equally fierce struggle was being waged in the courts over possession of the enormously valuable patent rights to barbed wire. An Illinois farmer named Glidden held the patent to the basic wire form which has dominated the market ever since, but every enterprising tinkerer tried to come up with his own version that would rake in some of the millions the burgeoning industry was reaping. Although Glidden triumphed in the courthouse, the simplicity of wire production and the lack of strict policing in the sparsely populated West led many small-time manufacturers to try and turn a profit producing "moonshine wire" in makeshift plants that could be packed up and moved out as soon as the inevitable Glidden representatives, armed with court orders, appeared on the scene. The relics of this period of freewheeling invention and production are still tacked to old fence posts across the prairie states.

◆ RANGE ◆

Throughout the country, with specimens found in every township from coast to coast. Early barbed wire came from the prairie states and it is there and in the West that most examples of its wildly inventive heyday will be found.

◆ WHERE TO LOOK ◆

Early samples of barbed wire are collectors' items today, with 1½ foot lengths commonly selling for $3 to $5 each; avid hunters rake the countryside for choice pieces. Fortunately, there is so much land and wire around that you'll be able to see plenty of undisturbed relics. Barbed wire can be found in almost any location that was farmed or ranched a century ago, but the oldest examples are in the prairie and western states. However, that is not carved in stone. Eastern and northern farmers jumped at the chance to rid themselves of the expense and burden of maintaining wooden fences, and it is likely that in those areas moonshine wire factories were regular interlopers on the Glidden patent as well.

Check along old fence lines for rotted posts still trailing strands of wire, and pay special attention to boundary trees (see Chapter 3, Plant Language) marking old property divisions. Often you'll discover a section of barbed wire that has been enveloped by the growing tree; protruding ends will give you an accurate signpost to the lie of the fence.

Early Barbed-Wire Types

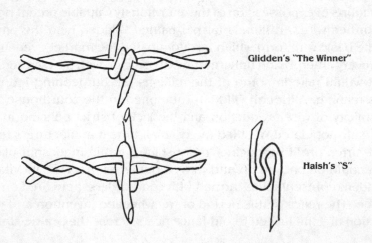

Glidden's "The Winner"

Haish's "S"

The first types of barbed wire manufactured had double-ended points loosely strung on a single wire. This unsatisfactory arrangement quickly gave way to the two-wire twist.

A second early attempt used common horseshoe nails bent around a plain wire; with a smaller gauge wire spiraled around both of them. Other quickly forgotten failures tried such solutions as stringing the barbs from Osage Orange hedges on wire.

Between 1868 and 1877 there were varied attempts to find a suitable wire, but the Glidden and Haish patents were the most widely used.

Scutt's Clip (Vicious)

Between 1876 and 1880, inventors thought the most effective wire was designed with "vicious" barbs which were razor-sharp and relied on pain to prevent stock from testing a barrier a second time. The cuts this wire inflicted left cattle vulnerable to screwworm infestation, which, in time, meant substantial losses. Subsequently vicious wire was removed from domestic production and only employed around prisons and battlegrounds.

Buckthorn (Obvious)

Between 1879 and 1884, and in reaction to vicious wire, many types of "obvious" wire were developed. While they pricked the wayward animal, they did not cut. Furthermore, they were designed to be easily seen by stock before contact was made. From 1884 up to the present "modified" wire has dominated production as the earlier and less effective types were weeded out, and as the Glidden patent was more effectively enforced, enabling the Glidden monopoly to basically control the market. Modified wire incorporated parts of each of the earlier versions and is still the wire of choice on countless properties.

37. NAILS

You've probably never pictured yourself eagerly stalking bent and discarded nails in old lumber. To most people they're simply mean-spirited hazards waiting to rip the clothing and flesh of innocent bystanders. In fact, nails are friendly trail markers that can help you determine a building's age with some degree of accuracy.

Before 1800, nails were valuable and distinctive artifacts. Many farmers spent part of the long winter months in the home manufacture of nails from nailrods purchased from a nearby iron furnace or traveling peddlar. Others relied on the local blacksmith's hammer.

Wrought-iron nails were the only ones available, each a different example of handwork at the forge. Their holding power was excellent, but the time and energy involved in their manufacture restricted their use to special tasks like affixing lathing or fastening door planks.

In sharp contrast to today's cavalier notions, handwrought nails were considered expensive materials and were never to be wasted. They were often used again and again, carefully kept track of and pulled from old construction when circumstances warranted it.

It's easy to spot a handwrought nail. The irregularity of its surface clearly shows the defining impact of repeated hammerblows. Since nails were fashioned from thin bars of iron, all four sides of the wrought nail taper to a point.

This difficult and limited manufacture—and use—of nails did not continue once the United States became an independent nation and it was clear that both the population and the pace of new construction were going to expand dramatically as settlement moved westward.

The earliest use of nail-cutting machinery was in the late 1700s and by the turn of the century no less than twenty-three patents relating to nail-cutting machines and their improvement had been granted in this country. Farmstead and local blacksmith production of wrought nails rapidly became a thing of the past.

Machine-made nails were cut from a flat sheet of iron, and tapered on only two sides. Between 1790 and 1830, nailheads were formed by repeated hammerblows and their irregular surfaces are obvious.

After 1830, refinements in the process of making nails produced cleanly stamped nailheads that were flat and smooth.

During the 1880s, wire nails came into widespread use, although the earliest examples were manufactured in New York during the early 1850s.

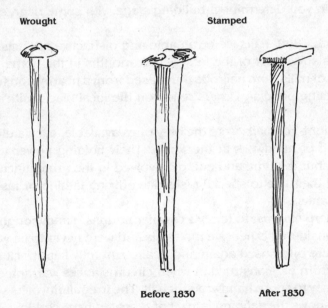

Wrought   Stamped

Before 1830   After 1830

38♦

POTTERY: ARTIFACT IDENTIFICATION

Utilitarian pottery was on the shelves of every American home. Bowls, pitchers, milk pans, crocks, pie plates, and a host of specialized forms created from clay were sold to meet the public's ever-present demand for basic creature comforts.

More often than not, the pottery found in any given area was of local manufacture. The long-distance shipment of finished pieces was expensive and liable to shatter profits as well as pots.

Pieces that surface some distance from the kiln where they were fired may have special histories. Their kiln could have been fortuitously located along a major waterway, which made cheap and safe haulage to distant markets quite possible. The pot might have been a cherished one and was carefully moved with the family's possessions, or it could have been part of a bride's dowry.

You might think that by examining local pottery you would be able to trace the history of past affluence, mobility, and cultural influences. Alas, it is not that simple.

The "collectibles" curse (from a historian's point of view) has been put on all early pottery of America. Pieces are zealously sought by dealers and individuals who forage the countryside. They are bought, removed from their original locations, traded, and generally admired. The preservation of these monuments of the American craftsman's work is surely commendable, but it does mean the proudly displayed piece you find in a colonial farmhouse could have started its journey in a far different time and place. As an interpretive clue, it is worthless.

The nature of pottery often makes it of questionable use as an artifact through which a date can be determined. Much of it was fashioned for prosaic, everyday use, and shaped to standard forms which were generally adopted because they suited the task at hand

and the potter's wheel. You can compare pottery thrown on a wheel to marked pieces in local collections for clues to its origin, but your best guess will remain only that. In the absence of a maker's stamp, molded pottery created in any one location is virtually indistinguishable from that produced elsewhere.

Nevertheless, you will find that a great deal of pottery can speak to you in an intelligible tongue. Pieces revealing their long and useful life through chipped rims, broken handles, cracks, or missing parts rarely fit the collector's image, and are often left to their own devices. You'll certainly come upon many of these waifs, resting on dusty shelves or reposing in refuse heaps. Even with its limitations, a working knowledge of the types of pottery, their geographical range, and their use as benchmarks can still be a profitable addition to your investigative arsenal.

◆   **REDWARE**   ◆

◆ RANGE: ◆

Mostly New England and the Middle Atlantic states. Some in the South, Midwest, and Far West prior to 1850 when redware was eclipsed by stoneware.

Redware is pottery made from the same run-of-the-mill clay that sufficed for common brick (see Chapter 14, Brickyards and Clayworks). Today, flowerpots are almost the only objects still fashioned from redware, but during the height of its popularity in the eighteenth and early nineteenth centuries, redware was used for everything from marbles to massive jugs. Clay for redware was common, but the fired pot was very fragile. You are far more apt to discover a nineteenth-century piece (or fragment) than an earlier one.

Some common redware items like trenchers and pie plates were hand-molded. Most of its production, however, was thrown on a potter's wheel, and more often than not it was the output of a single potter or a small shop. Decorations with coggle wheels, punches, or wavy lines created by holding sticks or awls to the revolving pottery are characteristic of items made before 1840.

Glazes were essential in the production of redware because of the clay's porous nature. Any piece intended to hold liquids had to be sealed with a fired glaze before it could be used.

Clear lead glazes were commonly employed, often with dire consequences from the lead poisoning they caused. A white clay called slip was used for decoration under the glaze; other colors, too, were popular. Manganese oxide produced black, favored in New England and New York for teapots. As potteries spread westward they carried this tradition to Illinois. Orange and brown glazes came from the use of iron. Copper imparted a mustardish green.

◆ STONEWARE ◆

A typical mid–1800's price list

◆ RANGE ◆

The whole country; early centers were in New York, New Jersey, and Pennsylvania where deposits of suitable clay were readily available. By the 1850s the Midwest had become the major center of production. Small operations were scattered throughout the South and West.

Stoneware was made from a special clay that fired at a much higher temperature than redware and, hence, produced an extremely durable product. (Purists will argue that stoneware is not considered pottery, and in the strict definition of both words, they are right. However, most people are not so technical. They think of stoneware as pottery, and for the purposes of this book, we choose to do so also.) Stoneware clay was comparatively rare and early production was limited to areas served by major waterways or close to kaolin deposits.

Anything that could be made from redware could also be made from stoneware clay, and with more lasting results. As soon as a national canal and rail system developed to the point where the transport of large quantities of clay was economically feasible, stoneware was used almost exclusively. By 1850 it was the major type of pottery found in the country.

◆ DISTINGUISHING FEATURES ◆

The only decorative material able to withstand the high (2200°) firing temperature of the stoneware kiln was cobalt, which fired a clear blue. Generally, the earlier the ware, the sparser and ruder the ornamental design brushed onto it. Pottery thrown before 1850 frequently sported only a couple of dabs of blue at the handle bases, or a very crude floral design.

During the second half of the nineteenth century the American passion for education left its mark on the potter's output. Day schools and penmanship classes proliferated and taught a country the niceties of elegantly flowing Spencerian script. Bird and animal designs were part of the rote exercises that carefully trained young hands in the control of the pen. A menagerie of freehand bluebirds, deer, and the like surfaced at potteries across the nation as artisans applied their newly acquired expertise. The major output of most stoneware kilns was heavy jugs and crocks. There is a simple technique you can use to obtain a quick estimate of their age. The tapering shape of the hand-thrown cylinder is readily spotted on jugs thrown before 1850 or so.

Early

After 1850, jugs were given straight sides. They were still thrown on the potter's wheel but plaster molds and scrapers insured uniformity.

Later

Much stoneware bears the imprint of its maker's stamp, routinely applied as a standard method of advertising. Though no date may be given, the city of origin will be established; further exploration in the library or contact with one of the many pottery collectors' clubs will probably fill you in on the working life of the pottery.

◆ BROWNWARE AND YELLOWWARE ◆

◆ RANGE ◆

Eastern and Midwestern states.

A middle ground between the lightness and fragility of redware and the ponderous durability of stoneware was found in brownware and yellowware. A 2000° kiln produced durable, lightweight pottery eminently suitable for everyday tableware.

Rockingham ware was named for the distinctive brown glaze achieved by using manganese and other metal salts. It was nearly always molded, often in fanciful patterns.

Yellowware rarely had any pretensions other than bands of decorative colors which enlivened its monochrome. Used exclusively for simple kitchenware, it was rarely signed or identified by a maker's imprint.

WALLPAPER

Decorators and renovators of old houses often shudder when they ponder the layers of wallpaper clinging to the walls. All they see is the tedious chore of removing the paper in order to reach the original surface.

It is a sadly limited viewpoint, much like the tunnel vision of restoration purists who consider a building properly done only when it is returned to its original state. But the imprints of succeeding generations of inhabitants are the very marks that turn buildings into living, historically vital structures.

Wallpaper can conjure up visions of the dwelling that sheltered earlier tenants and allow you to capture the flavor of their lives. A small piece of faded wallpaper discovered under a peeling layer of dingy paint can transport you back in time to a grander domestic past.

♦ ## RANGE ♦

Throughout the nation; arriving as towns developed and merchant and professional classes evolved.

◆ WHERE TO LOOK ◆

Your most likely hunting places are the solid houses built by successful settlers who had long since shed the rude habitations of the frontier. Middle-class and upper-class houses, whether of farmer or merchant prince, regularly used wallpaper to embellish their living spaces.

Entryways, passageways, and halls merit your close observation. They were the locations most often papered over.

◆ DISTINGUISHING FEATURES ◆

The earliest wallpapers of colonial America were reserved for the houses of the well-to-do. Papers imported from England, France, and China were expensive frills, at home only in the environs of the civilized town house or the stately country manor.

As the population increased and a significant middle class developed in towns and villages, the heightened demand for wallpaper brought prices within reach of those who were climbing up the social ladder but hadn't yet gained the more stratified rungs.

All wallpaper made before 1835 or so was handcrafted and pieced together from individually printed sheets. Horizontal seams at regular intervals are your certain indications of early paper. Sometimes you can persuade them to reveal themselves—even when they are topped with later paper—by shining a flashlight sideways along the wall surface. Any irregularities in the flat plane of the wall will be thrown into shadowed relief. Other signs of a paper's handmade origin are watermarks, irregular and ragged edges, and the unmistakable impressions left by the wire screens of the papermaker.

The French had a virtual monopoly on wallpaper sold in this country between 1800 and 1870. Indeed, their designs sold very well in the American marketplace. Wealthy Americans in the late eighteenth and early nineteenth century were concerned with the forms of their houses and *architecture papers*, which created two-dimensional columns and friezes in formal interiors, became the state of the art for interior design. During the early decades of the 1800s, papers mimicking stone or brickwork gradually captured center stage in the architectural pantheon.

Between 1800 and 1850, *landscape papers* were fervently purchased by the moderately prosperous merchant or professional who was decorating a new home. These French productions were realistic and detailed, presenting scenes from both the European and American landscape. They broadened the world for the proud householder and fit conveniently right above the chair rail where they could best be appreciated.

During the 1840s, the papermaking industry underwent the industrial revolution and emerged mechanized and capable of inexpensive mass production. Practically overnight, wallpaper became a cheap and, hence, most transportable commodity; it could easily be sent to the frontier. Enterprising merchants found it a profitable addition to their general line of merchandise. Individual families of settlers often carried a few rolls westward as part of their freight of aspirations and dreams of a better life. Odd bits of wallpaper left over after installation, made those westward journeys as well, gracing, as they did, the interiors of countless chests and trunks.

Machine-made wallpaper was less impressive than its handmade predecessor. It revealed small-scale repeating designs and its colors were relatively thin. But few people, recently able to bedeck their modest homes with such marks of civilization, cared a jot. Wallpaper's status as a universal American artifact was assured.

APPENDIX

◆ ARCHITECTURAL GLOSSARY ◆

ADOBE   Sun-dried brick commonly used for construction in the Southwest.

ANCHOR IRON   An iron plate, bar, or ring used to hold a masonry wall securely to a wooden beam. Often decoratively shaped. Very common in nineteenth-century brick construction.

ANTHEMION   A common Greek-influenced architectural ornament based on the honeysuckle flower.

ARCHITRAVE   The lowest part of a classical entablature; resting directly on the columns. Also the molding that frames a door or window.

ASHLAR   Stone that has been shaped into large, regular blocks. Can be coursed or randomly laid.

BALLOON FRAME   Framing using small dimension lumber like two-by-fours that are nailed together.

BARGEBOARD   Also known as vergeboard. The board covering the rafters at the gable end of the roof. Sometimes very decoratively carved and jigsawed.

BATTENS   Boards of varying dimensions used to build simple doors or to provide siding.

BEEHIVE OVEN   A domed bake oven projecting from the outside wall of a house. Seventeenth and eighteenth century.

BELVEDERE   A turret or tower built to provide a view.

BRACKET   A brace used between a vertical section and a horizontal member lying above it. Often used decoratively rather than structurally.

BRICK BONDS   Methods of holding construction together by alternately overlapping the long and short brick ends.

BRICK NOGGING   Brick infill used between wall studs for insulation. Usually of poorly fired and otherwise worthless brick.

CANTILEVER   A beam, joist, or bracket projecting from a wall without exterior support; held by the weight on its interior length.

CAPE COD STYLE   A New England colonial style with one story, central chimney, and large ridge roof that comes down to ceiling level.

CAPITAL   The top part of a column or pilaster.

CARPENTER GOTHIC   A loose term for any Victorian Gothic Revival wooden house with decorative jigsawed, carved, or turned adornment.

CASEMENT   A hinged window that opens outward.

CATSLIDE   Southern term for the New England Saltbox lean-to house.

CLAPBOARD Overlapping siding of sawed or riven boards laid horizontally.

COLUMN A round vertical supporting member.

CORNER BOARD A vertical siding board nailed to the corner post of a post-and-beam house.

CORNICE A roof-line molding; the topmost section of an entablature.

CROSS GABLE A gable that lies parallel to the roof's ridge-line.

CUPOLA A small, often windowed structure, that rises from the top of a building.

DENTILS Small rectangular blocks forming a running ornament beneath a cornice.

DORMER A window that projects from a roof and illuminates the attic space.

DRIP COURSE A course of masonry that stands out from a wall and sends water past the surface immediately below it.

DUTCH DOOR A door bisected horizontally across the middle, and hinged so that either the top or bottom half can be opened.

DUTCH OVEN A deep cast-iron pot. Not an attached oven.

ENGLISH BOND See brick bonds.

ENTABLATURE The architrave, frieze, and cornice carried by columns in a classical arrangement.

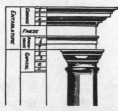

EYEBROW WINDOW   The low rectangular window set in the architrave in a Greek Revival house. Also known as a lie-on-your-stomach window.

FANLIGHT   A semicircular window set above a door.

FIXED SASH   A window that cannot be opened.

FLEMISH BOND   See brick bonds.

FRIEZE   The middle part of an entablature between cornice and architrave.

GABLE   The end wall beneath a pitched roof.

GAMBREL ROOF   A roof with two pitches on either side of its ridge.

GINGERBREAD   Decorative jigsawed or scroll-sawed, under-eave ornament on Victorian buildings.

GREEK FRET   A mazelike, continuous ornament.

HALF-TIMBERING   Post-and-beam construction with the framing visible on the outside walls.

HIPPED ROOF   A roof that slopes back equally on all four sides.

JAMB   An upright piece framing a doorway, window, or fireplace opening.

JOIST   A small timber used to support a ceiling or floor.

LIGHTS   Window panes.

LINTEL   A beam of wood, iron, stone, etc. spanning an opening in a wall or between two pillars.

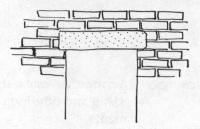

MANSARD ROOF   All four sides have two pitches, with the bottom much steeper than the top.

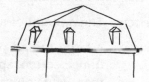

MULLION   A heavy vertical dividing bar in a window.

MUNTIN   Thin pieces of wood or metal that hold window lights in place.

ORIEL WINDOW   A small rectangular bay window supported by brackets.

PALLADIAN WINDOW   A tripartite window with a large arched central light and two lower ones crowned with entablatures.

PEDIMENT   The triangular space formed by the gable end of a two-pitched roof; a similar form used in classical architecture as decoration over windows, doors, and the like.

PENT ROOF   A narrow eaveslike shed roof projecting from a wall and offering protection from the elements.

PILASTER   A vertical, rectangular pillar simulating a classical column and projecting only slightly from a wall.

PITCH   The amount of slope to a roof.

PORTICO   A large roofed porch over a building's entrance, often sporting full classical pediment and columns.

QUOINS   Large blocks of stone or wood set to form the corners of a building. Can provide structural reinforcement or be purely decorative.

RUBBLE   Stones given minimal artificial shaping.

RUSTICATION   Rough-surfaced stonework formed by tooling.

SALTBOX HOUSE   A one-and-a-half or two-story house with a distinctive long, rear roof that is normally presented to the north. Known in the South as a catslide house.

SASH A window frame that slides up or down to open.

SCROLLWORK Decorative wooden designs cut with a scroll saw.

SHAKES Large, split-wood shingles.

SIDELIGHTS Small fixed panes of glass along the sides of a doorway.

STRING COURSE A projecting horizontal band that runs across a building's wall. Normally of plain or molded brick.

SUMMER BEAM A massive beam that is the principal support of floors in post-and-beam construction. Short floor joists are laid at right angles to it.

TENON The projecting point of a wooden beam that fits into the morticed socket of another to form a strong connection.

TRANSOM A flat rectangular window above a doorway.

VERGEBOARD See bargeboard.

◆ SELECTED BIBLIOGRAPHY ◆

Small local history collections in town and college libraries contain much of the most useful, entertaining, and detailed doorways to the past. County histories written for the 1876 Centennial, old city directories, and the like are invaluable. There you'll also stumble across rarely opened books about local histories sure to be full of revelation about specific topics.

Here is a far-from-complete listing of books with a wider scope. Get to know them, and you'll gain the solid historical background that makes rewarding forays into the past regular adventures.

◆ PART I ◆

Clay, Grady. *Close-Up: How to Read the American City.* Chicago: University of Chicago Press, 1980.

Hart, John Fraser. *The Look of the Land.* Englewood Cliffs, N.J.: Prentice-Hall, 1975.

———— and Raitz, Karl. *Cultural Geography on Topographical Maps.* New York: Wiley, 1975.

Johnson, Hildegard Binder. *Order upon the Land.* New York: Oxford University Press, 1976.

Reps, John W. *The Making of Urban America—A history of city planning in the United States.* Princeton, N.J.: Princeton University Press, 1965.

Sloane, Eric. *Our Vanishing Landscape.* New York: Ballantine Books, 1976.

Stewart, George R. *Names on the Land.* New York: Houghton Mifflin, 1967.

◆ PART II ◆

Coolidge, John. *Mill and Mansion.* New York: Russell and Russell, 1967.

Drago, Mary Sinclair. *Canal Days in America.* New York: Bramhall House, 1972.

Hunter, Louis C. *Waterpower—A History of Industrial Power in the United States,* Volume I. Charlottesville, Va.: University Press of Virginia, 1979.

Ketchum, William C., Jr. *The Pottery and Porcelain Collector's Handbook—A Guide to Early American Ceramics from Maine to California.* New York: Funk & Wagnalls, 1971.

Rawson, Marion Nicholl. *Handwrought Ancestors.* New York: Dutton, 1936.

Ries and Laughton. *A History of the Clayworking Industry in the United States.* New York: Wiley, 1909.

Rose, Albert C. *Historic American Roads.* New York: Crown, 1976.

Sande, Theodore Anton. *Industrial Archeology.* New York: Penguin, 1976.

Schlereth, Thomas J. *Artifacts and the American Past.* Nashville: The American Assn. for State and Local History, 1980.

Weitzman, David. *Traces of the Past—A Field Guide to Industrial Archaeology.* New York: Scribner's, 1980.

_____. *Underfoot—An Everyday Guide to Exploring the American Past.* New York: Scribner's, 1976.

Young, Otis E., Jr. *Western Mining.* Norman, Okla.: University of Oklahoma Press, 1970.

◆ PART III ◆

There are literally hundreds of architectural guides available. These are particularly easy to read and widely available.

Rifkind, Carole. *A Field Guide to American Architecture.* New York: New American Library, 1980.

Whiffen, Marcus. *American Architecture since 1780: A Guide to the Styles.* Cambridge, Mass.: MIT Press, 1969.

Wrenn, Tony P. and Malloy, Elizabeth D. *America's Forgotten Architecture.* New York: Pantheon, 1976.

◆ PART IV ◆

There is a large body of works on barns and farmhouses readily available. You might start with the following.

Halstead, Byron D. *Barns, Sheds, and Outbuildings.* Brattleboro, Vt. Stephen Green Press, 1977 (originally published 1881).

Kauffman, Henry J. *The American Farmhouse.* New York: Hawthorne, 1975.

Klamkin, Charles. *Barns—Their History, Preservation, and Restoration.* New York: Hawthorne, 1973.

◆ PART V ◆

Ketchum, William C., Jr. *The Pottery and Porcelain Collector's Handbook—A Guide to Early American Ceramics from Maine to California.* New York: Funk & Wagnalls, 1971.

————. *A Treasury of American Bottles.* New York: Bobbs-Merrill, 1975.

Klamkin, Marian. *The Collector's Book of Bottles.* New York: Dodd Mead, 1971.

Lynn, Catherine. *Wallpaper in America—from the 17th Century to World War I.* New York: W.W. Norton, 1980.

McCallum, Henry D. and Frances T. *The Wire that Fenced the West.* Norman, Okla.: University of Oklahoma Press, 1970.

Southworth, Susan and Michael. *Ornamental Ironwork.* Boston: David R. Godine, 1978.

INDEX